DIVING GUIDE TO THE

BRITISH ISL___
AND NORTHERN
EUROPE

SWAN·HILL
PRESS

BRITISH ISLES AND NORTHERN EUROPE

Text
Nils Aukan
Stefan Baehr
Paul Kay
Harry Klerks
Ulkira Kroon
Inge Lennmark
Patrick Mouton
Mark Webster
Carsten Werner
Lawson Wood

Editorial coordination
Livio Bourbon

Graphic design
Luana Gobbo

Illustrations of the dives
Mariano Valsesia

Maps
Elisabetta Ferrero

Fish charts:
Texts
Angelo Mojetta

Illustrations
Monica Falcone

Translation
C.T.M., Milan

A

B

I Wherever there is a tidal current you will encounter filter feeders such as these attractive plumose anemones (Metridium senile). This species is most often found on the sheer walls of offshore reefs or on wrecks in exposed waters.

2-3 Jewel Anemones (Corynactis viridis) adorn many of the exposed bedrock seabeds off the whole of Ireland's West coast.

4 top A large edible crab (Cancer pargurus) grazes on soft corals (Alcyonium digitatum). This species is rathar common in northern Europe waters.

4 bottom The sheer walls of the reef are densely overgrown with fields of plumose anemones (Metridium senile) that come in a variety of delicate colours.

Contents

INTRODUCTION

A - Cancer pagurus
lies perfectly
camouflaged against
the rugged bottom.

B - The angler fish is
common on both sandy
sea beds and on the
reefs. It is a highly
prized catch for the
trawler fishermen, but
only the tail of this ugly
fish is eaten. It is truly
delicious!

B

C

Global diving travel has become increasingly easy over the last decade providing quick access to a growing number of tropical and exotic destinations. There is now a temptation, particularly for European divers, to look only towards these distant locations and perhaps ignore the wealth of diving variety we have here right on our own doorstep. For many the image of the seas in Northern Europe may be of dark grey or green cold waters pounding the coastline during relentless storms. Whilst this does occur during the winter months, it is a misleading image. When you dive into these cooler waters you will be amazed at the rich array of colourful marine life and many familiar species which have relations in tropical climes. This guide covers an immensely large area within Northern Europe which includes the Atlantic Ocean, the Irish Sea, the North Sea, Norwegian Sea and Baltic Sea from the Bay of Biscay to the isolated splendour of the Norwegian fjords. Nations with coastlines in these waters, offer a tremendous range of coastal and undersea topography, marine habitats for wide variety of flora and fauna, with climates ranging from temperate in the south to near Arctic in the north. You can choose to dive from sandy beaches and bays, towering cliffs, offshore islands and pinnacles or within the shelter of deep fjords and lochs. Underwater you will find the leafy glades of the kelp forests, open sandy plains, gullies, caves and caverns and the exhilaration of sheer drop-offs and cliff faces. The waters throughout this area are strongly influenced by tides and currents. Diurnal tides create extremely strong currents - up to 6-7 knots in many areas featuring great water

A

movement. A rise and fall of 8m or more is not unusual during spring tides in areas such as southern Brittany and the west coast of Scotland. It is, naturally, this very movement of sea water that brings in the nutrients on which the rich marine life survives. In some areas these tides will, of course, dictate when and where you can dive safely. Drift diving in the current is popular, but should only be attempted in the right conditions and with the correct preparation and surface cover. Otherwise it is generally best to dive during periods of slack tide or when neap tides prevail. The other great influence on many of these northern coastal areas is provided by the Gulf Stream running in from warmer Atlantic waters. This warmer current splits around the south-western reaches of England and then continues northwards to become the North Atlantic Drift as it reaches the fjords of Norway that it helps to keep ice-free during the winter months. The effects of these warmer waters are reflected in marine life throughout the region. Even in these temperate waters you will find species of soft corals, hydro corals, gorgonian corals and seemingly endless varieties of brightly coloured anemones, tube worms, sponges and sea squirts. There is also colour amongst the fish life particularly on the reefs where you will find bright red gurnards, rainbow coloured cuckoo wrasse, camouflaged scorpionfish and many exotic looking blennies and gobies. The sandy environments around the reef and close to river estuaries, are home to plaice, sole, turbot and several species of ray whilst in the open waters offshore, you will find shoals of mackerel, herring, pilchards and cod. There are even several species of shark, common throughout the region, but your most likely encounter will be with that harmless giant, the basking shark, which can be seen in great numbers feeding on the springtime plankton blooms. Marine habitats world-wide are under threat from man's pollution and these northern seas are no

exception. Fortunately, many governments are recognising the fragile balance of the marine environment and some proactive moves are underway to regulate dumping and overfishing. There are already some examples of this protection in the form of marine reserves and designated protection areas aiming at preservation of these seas for future generations. For now, we have collected together in this guide the best dive sites on offer, in areas where there is little industry and pollution levels are so low that it is still possible to admire the marine world as nature intended it to be.

E

F

E - The first plancton blooms take place in the late spring and early summer throughout the North Sea. These are closely followed by large numbers of basking sharks (Cetorhinus maximus) that feed on these small planctonic organisms. Some reach 4-5 metres in length but are totally harmless.

F - The common sea urchin (Echinus esculentus) come in striking colours and are found grazing on algae on the reef.

Planning

A - Cold Scandinavian waters offer plenty of opportunities for breathtaking wreck dives.

B- A diver ventures into a kelp forest off the Norwegian coast. Kelp or laminaria, is very widespread in Nordic seas.

C - Close encounters of the bizarre kind are not uncommon in northern waters. Here a diver engages in a tête-à-tête with a rather forbidding-looking phylum Coelenterata, class Scyphozoa.

D - Below 15 metres, the laminaria hyperborea disappears to make way for invertebrates and other fixed marine creatures, such as sponges (Cliona celata).

D iving is an immensely popular sport in northern Europe and is constantly expanding. Divers are particularly well served by the number of diving centres and shops that have sprung up along coastlines and further inland to serve the cities and certain land-locked diving sites. The most reliable information on diving in your area of interest, will surely be found in the national diving magazines, in which most diving and training centres advertise their services. Many of these magazines and centres have now established websites on the Internet that has become an invaluable research tool, providing easy communications with each location as well as general information on the host country and surrounding areas. You may also wish to consider visiting one of the many diving and water sports exhibitions in which many of the major centres and travel companies participate. Some of the best known shows include 'Boot' in Dusseldorf, the Diver International Dive Show in London and Birmingham, the Antibes Festival, the Salon de la Plongée in Paris, the Duiksportbeurs in Houten and there are many others to choose from.

In order to dive anywhere in northern Europe you must be suitably qualified by a recognised training agency and have sufficient experience of the type of conditions you expect to experience at your chosen location. Many diving centres will offer training packages for dry suit diving, drift diving in current,

B

deep diving and diving to wrecks, etc. Each nation will have its own national diving federation and many of the diving centres will be agents for one of the commercial training organisations (such as PADI, NAUI, SSI). Most qualifications have an equivalent grade with other organisations, but one of the most internationally recognised is the CMAS star grading system. You can obtain a CMAS 'C' card through your national diving federation or alternatively check with the diving centre you will be using to ensure your qualification will be recognised. Even if you have these qualifications, many centres will also require you to undertake a preliminary test dive, particularly if your experience is mostly in warmer waters. Again, check with the diving centre first and always carry your qualifications and current log book.

If you travel with your own boat be sure to check with the local harbour and coast guard authorities for any national safety regulations that you may have to comply with, e.g. flares, radios, EPRB beacon, life rafts etc. Also enquire about local radio communication procedures for normal liaison and emergency contact in the event of a marine or diving emergency. If you plan to dive independently it is particularly important to know what action to take in the event of decompression sickness. Also add to your list, details of local tide tables and maritime weather forecasts for the sea area you will be

E - At certain times of year the visibility can be impressive. When conditions are good divers can explore large areas of the reef using a boat.

A

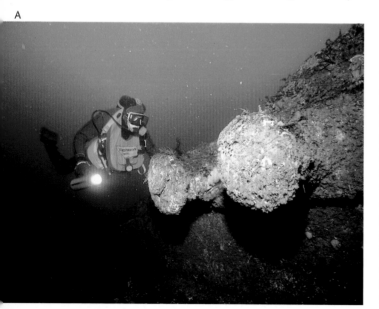

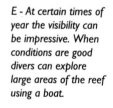

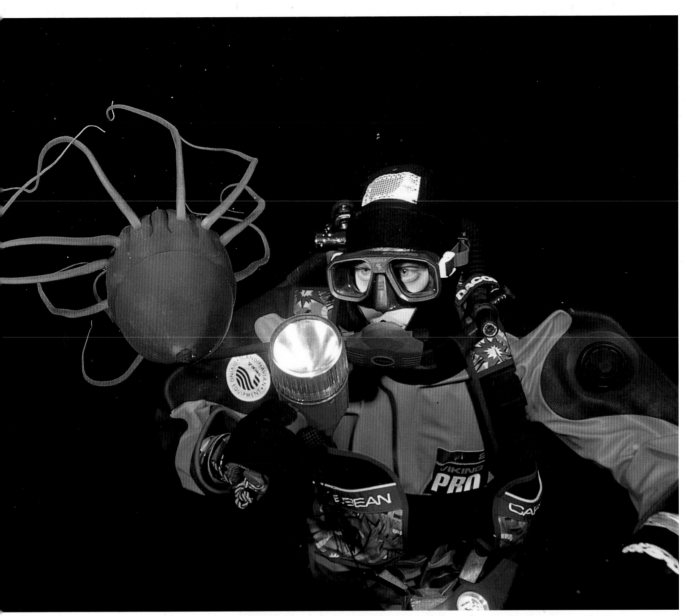

D

E

diving in. This check-list should be adapted to suit the size of your group and the type of diving you plan on doing, but much of the information and many of the contact details can now be found on the Internet – a great time-saver when researching an expedition. Divers often travel within Europe with all their own equipment including cylinders. Most nations will operate an compulsory testing scheme for pressure cylinders and you may be required to prove that your cylinder has been tested to an acceptable European standard before a diving centre will fill it. Once again, check with the centre to ensure that your equipment complies. Similarly, some nations favour the 'A' clamp style of attaching the regulator first stage to the cylinder whilst others adopt the DIN screw fitting. When you are hiring equipment you must ensure that it will be compatible with your own system and also check if you will be

required to carry an alternative air source, either an octopus regulator or a totally separate pony cylinder supply. Diving is possible all year round in all areas but, naturally, winter diving can be more of a lottery due to the potentially stormy conditions, although there are a number of areas, such as the Norwegian fjords, that offer sheltered waters in most conditions. While Summertime may be the best time to plan a diving expedition since the weather is more predictable, winter

diving offers amazing visibility and sea conditions, between storms. The seasons also have a dramatic effect on water temperature - the coldest months are February and March, after the sea has cooled during the autumn and winter. Sea temperatures can range from 14-17°c in the south of the region in the summer to a bone numbing 4-5°c in the north in the winter.

Equipment

A - Preparing to dive in the Baltic Sea. The equipment required for this dive must be suitable for cold water diving. This means a dry suit and two regulators that must be independent from each other. A spare torchlight should be carried on all visits to underwater wrecks.

B - A Royal Navy diver is preparing his rebreather before diving on the Royal Oak, in Scotland, to examine her hull for signs of deterioration and oil leakage.

In order to get the most out of your diving and to ensure comfort and safety, you must choose the correct equipment to dive in these conditions. In the summer months, it is possible to dive throughout the region in a good quality semi-dry wetsuit (perhaps 6-8mm in thickness) but for real comfort in all seasons, and for longer duration or deeper dives, the best choice is a drysuit. When choosing your drysuit you must weigh the advantages and disadvantages of a membrane suit and a neoprene drysuit. Membrane suits are perhaps lighter, offer greater freedom of movement on the surface and maybe require less lead on your weight belt. However, they have no real thermal protective qualities, so you must wear a heavy under suit, and they provide no

C - Drysuit clad divers kitting up on the banks of the marine but river-like Menai Strait, in Wales.

inherent buoyancy, should the suit flood. They can also give your flesh a nasty squeeze if you do not equalise the suit correctly or perhaps wear too little on your weight belt. The neoprene choice has the advantage of thermal insulation in the material and offers the inherent buoyancy qualities of a wetsuit, which makes the suit somewhat safer if it floods. But, although you may wear less thermal underwear you will have to wear a heavier weight belt to overcome the buoyancy of the suit. There is a third choice of a compressed neoprene material which is now popular. This material produces a hybrid suit which offers some of the qualities of both the membrane and the full neoprene suit. An educated choice means you must try as many combinations as possible to find which is most comfortable for you and the type of diving that you undertake.

In order to keep your head and hands warm whilst diving, a well-fitting hood and gloves are essential. For very cold water diving, you may consider a hood with a face seal which will reduce the amount of cold water flushing and perhaps a pair of dry gloves which will increase the duration of your dive.

Regardless of the suit you choose, you will need to wear an additional buoyancy compensating device. Although it is possible to dive with a drysuit and use the suit inflation system to trim your buoyancy, it is not safe practice and you will be at risk of over inflating your suit which may lead to an uncontrolled ascent or an inversion if too much air collects in the legs of the suit. The suit inflation should only be used to trim the compression in the suit

B

C

until it is comfortable and your buoyancy at depth is then controlled using your BCD. This will minimise the risk of air migration in the suit and position buoyancy where it is most effective for in-water stability, that is to say, around the torso and the scuba tank. There are many BCD systems to choose from, ranging from traditional horse collar jackets to waistcoats and wing systems. Some of these have emergency inflation systems, secondary breathing systems or integral weight systems, but once again the choice depends largely on personal taste, so try as many designs as possible. The one feature you should seek out is a strong construction rather than the lighter tropical BCD's now available for the travelling diver.

There are a huge number of demand valves available on the market today and although some of these are very high performance valves, there are few if any which could be said to be of poor design. In making a choice, you must imagine the type of conditions that you will be diving in. Will it be very cold water in the winter with the attendant danger of freezing in the first stage, or will you be working in very strong currents and therefore need high volume delivery or perhaps, you will be in deep water and therefore require low breathing resistance? Many dive shops will lend or rent you a selection of demand valves to try or perhaps you can borrow differing demand valves to test from fellow club members. Since the ergonomic features of some valves vary markedly – so much so, that some are more suitable for lady divers (small mouthpiece) or perhaps for

photographers (a low profile second stage) – you may not want to make a choice based solely on valve performance. Many modern designs have the anti-freeze feature in the first stage as standard, but if not this is normally available as an option and is well worth having unless you are absolutely certain you will not use the valve in very cold conditions.

Even when you are diving in perfect conditions you must always concentrate on diving safely. In addition to your diving suit and life support system, there are certain other accessories that many divers consider as essential. Using a diving computer simplifies your dive planning and will enable you to plan multiple dives or do decompression dives, whether specifically planned or forced as a result of overstaying your time at depth. You should also carry a surface marker 'sausage' buoy to assist location by your cover boat at the end of a dive or during a safety stop. If you are drift diving it is often best to carry a buoy with a reel in order to mark your position on the surface throughout the dive. Even when dives are well planned, currents can often surprise you by not behaving as predicted and you can be carried significant distances both underwater and on the surface, if you are not picked up immediately at the end of a dive. Another worthwhile accessory is a flasher beacon which can be attached to your BCD as an emergency item or for use during night dives. Northern waters can often be dark either due to restricted visibility or depth, so a good quality torch should complete your equipment ensemble and prepare you for most conditions.

Photography

A,B - The marine species of the cold Norwegian waters have no reason to envy their tropical cousins when it comes to beauty and colour. Reduced sunlight and water transparency, however, tend to make wide-angled photography difficult and most underwater photographers in these waters used macro-lenses.

When it comes to the abundance of splendidly coloured subjects for underwater photographers, these waters can rival the tropics. The equipment required for successful underwater photography is quite the same in temperate and colder waters. Bear in mind however, that in colder waters, you may be wearing heavy neoprene gloves that could considerably hamper your handling of the camera, especially if the camera or casing has small controls. Some manufacturers have recognised this problem and there are several models on the market that can accommodate spacer blocks on the handles or base plates, to create more space for gloved hands.

As always, you must make sure that the techniques you use are suited to prevailing underwater conditions. Although visibility can be excellent in some areas at the right time of the year, it does tend to be poorer than in tropical or Mediterranean waters and as a result you may find yourself shooting more macro than wide-angle. The colour of the water will also differ from warmer climates being more greenish than deep blue and in general, light levels will be lower. Both these factors will affect your choice of film when the conditions are right for wide-angle – perhaps a faster film speed and an emulsion which produces warmer colours. If you can afford it, it may perhaps be best to carry two camera systems, so that you can either select the lens most suited to prevailing conditions or perhaps even dive with both systems, in unpredictable temperate waters.

Even with the best of visibility, you will often find some heavy particle suspension which can cause back scatter,

A

B

C

C - Good visibility, spectacular scenery and plentiful subject matter make the Aran Islands, in Ireland, an excellent area for photographers and videographers

E - Good lighting is essential for sharply contrasted images and to bring out the wondrous colours of underwater creatures.

D - Underwater photography is popular even in the temperate waters of Northern Europe. Some species of fish are as brightly coloured as their tropical cousins, but all require the same patience if you want a close-up.

D

E

if you do not position your flash guns carefully. In order to minimise the risk of back scatter, you should aim your flash towards the subject at an oblique angle of approximately 45° so that any light reflected by the particles is reflected towards the flash and not the lens.

There are many species of small reef fish, crustaceans, anemones, soft corals, tube worms and nudibranchs that make excellent macro subjects. You can use an amphibious camera system (such as the Motormarine or Nikonos) with an extension tube to capture these subjects or choose a macro lens with an SLR in a casing that extends the flexibility of your system, allowing you to photograph larger subjects on the same dive.

For wide-angle photography you should aim to be as close to your subject as possible. For this you will need a lens of 20mm focal length at least, but a fish eye lens is almost perfection as you can move in to a few centimetres from your subject and still cover a huge picture area. Using a balanced lighting technique is most effective and will produce a soft green background to your wide angle photographs.

Just as in the tropics, you will find that some marine life is very approachable and easy to photograph whilst other species are wary and shy. You need to adopt the skills of a hunter for some fish species or be prepared to wait patiently until you are accepted by your subject. Fish which use camouflage for attracting prey or for protection, are normally very easy to approach and photograph in

close-up. Scorpionfish, anglerfish, flatfish and cuttlefish are all very approachable and rewarding to photograph. Others, such as the members of the wrasse family, are more naturally inquisitive and will approach the photographer confidently posing for a portrait. Open water and shoaling species of fish often require a measure of luck for a successful photographic encounter. Diving on wrecks will generally increase your chance of success as species such as pouting, pollack, cod and ling are attracted to the protection and dark recesses of ship wrecks. This also makes them attractive to anglers and commercial fishermen, so be alert for

fishing lines and nets when swimming around wrecks.

Invertebrate life is of course much easier to photograph in both close-up and wide angle. Temperate reefs are extremely colourful and you can produce some stunning vistas when visibility is good and the sun shines. If conditions are not perfect concentrate on the intricate detail of anemones, tube worms and corals or consider taking silhouettes which can often produce stunning results. Whatever your choice, there is always a worthwhile subject in these cooler northern seas, as you can see in the pages of this guide to some of the finest sites on offer.

NORVEGIAN
SEA

NARVIK

KRISTIANSUND

VEVANGSTRØMMEN
AALESUND

Oslo
Stockholm

SAPPEMEER

TROLLESKÄR AND
STENSKÄR

NORTH
SEA

BALTIC
SEA

A – Kelp forest, (Laminaria), is common on rocks and islands facing the open sea. Kelp can grow up to height of 4 metres, and can be found at depths of up to 25 metres below the surface. The stems provide shelter for juvenile fish and crabs. A whole marine world comes to life under the kelp roof.

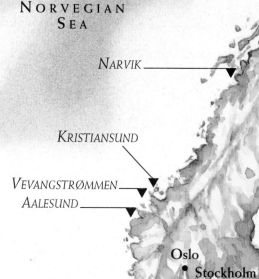

DIVING IN NORWAY

Southern Norway offers good diving sites, interspersed along both sides of the Oslo fjord, to the Swedish border. Visibility here is poorer than on Norway's western coast, but the marine life here is rich in fish. Visibility ranges between 3-4 m and 10-15 m. Diving is not possible in the Oslo fjord in winter, when thick ice covers the inner parts of the fjord and bays.

The eastern side of the Oslo fjord, from Tjøme to Kristiansand S, also offers good diving sites featuring rich underwater life and wrecks. As a general rule however, the best diving sites in Scandinavia are located along the western Norwegian coast, from Egersund up to the islands of Smøla and Hitra, off Trondheim. Crowds of European diving enthusiasts flock here in the summer. The fish and other marine species encountered in northern Norway are slightly less than on the other coasts, but all the species present in these waters are abundant. The underwater landscape is wild and visibility is generally very good. The Gulf Stream coming across the Atlantic, bending North along the Norwegian coastline ensures that the waters off the western coast are relatively warm and free of ice throughout the year. In winter, ice forms only in the deepest fjords, since cold rivers empty fresh water into them.

Summer surface temperatures range between 12 and 18°C with a drop of between 2 and 5 degrees in winter. At

B - Flatfish (Microstomus kitt), are common under the kelp, close to hard bottoms. Its mottled brown colour allows it to blend into the background.

C - Multicoloured soft corals (Alcyonum digitatum) as well as plumose anemomes, (Metridium senile) on a vertical rock face.

C

the bottom, located at a depth of 15 to 20 m, temperature swings are more contained with winter temperatures of about 7 to 5°C. Dry suits are advisable all the year round, although a thick wet suit could be used in summer at depths of up to 20-25 m. Marine life abounds under the surface. The sandy bottom is inhabited by crabs and various types of flounder, such as plaice, sole, brill and turbot. Schooling fish, especially coalfish, can be encountered in shallows and on the fringes of currents, down to depths of 20-30 metres. Pollack and codfish are common in the shallows. The fish hide amongst the large laminaria kelp facing the open sea. Diving under a kelp roof is truly an unforgettable experience. The stems are home to algae, sponges, and hydroids whereas between the hapteater (root filaments), you will find small crabs, squat lobsters

and blennies. Life under a kelp roof is so different from life above, it seems almost as though the kelp creates a whole new world. Each and every inch of fjord walls and drop-offs is covered with interesting marine creatures. It is not unknown for new species to be discovered here. Naturally, the long Norwegian coastline provides a great deal of other diving opportunities. The areas mentioned here, however, are particularly rich in good diving sites. These sites are also more accessible by road, air and sea than other remoter sites. With such a long coastline, featuring deep in-cutting fjords, the underwater landscape is full of breathtaking rock faces. Since fjords extend up to seven or eight hundred metres below the surface, so be sure to keep an eye on your depth gauge or computer! When visibility is optimal, from August to November, it is easy to

get carried away and venture too far down. Losing stability in deep-sea conditions against a race face can be fatal, since it is a long, long way to the bottom! The coastline features thousands of rocks, reefs and small islands that provide sheltered diving sites when the wind gets rough. In Norway, excellent dives can be undertaken even in storm conditions, without any loss of visibility! If you are amongst those who enjoy the thrill of diving into uncharted waters into which no one has ventured so far, Norway is literally bursting with opportunity. There are plenty of sites no one has ever tried. Before venturing into such waters however, always obtain full information about possible weather conditions, the best point of entry, recommended safety precautions,

A

may look, you can only watch them and photograph. Although spearfishing is allowed on most species, local diving centres tend to prohibit spearfishing around centres so as to encourage a diver-friendly attitude in the fish population. Salmon are protected under special laws and cannot be spearfished. Plaice is protected in the spring, during the spawning season. All visiting divers are required to comply with Norwegian laws protecting wrecks, especially historical wrecks. All wrecks over a hundred years of age are protected under specific laws and toying around with ancient wrecks is not tolerated. Penalties for such offences include imprisonment, a fine and the confiscation of the diving boat and all diving equipment.

life on
their minds. These waters are perfect for the preservation of wrecks. The area around Stockholm and the bigger cities is crowded with wrecks. Tens of thousands of steel freighters, wooden ships and warships, many of them perfectly preserved thanks to the absence of ship worm and rust.
In the southern parts of Sweden, a mix of the brackish Baltic Sea and the salty waters of the West coast gives divers both the opportunity of a more vivid marine life (mussels, eels, codfish) and a variety of sunken ships along the shores. Most divers head for the western coast. The salty waters of the Atlantic Ocean and the Gulf stream have made this area a perfect spot for animals and plants, since the area is exposed to the sometimes

B

currents, tides, re-entry, etc. It is not always possible to come up with fixed rules to be followed since dive patterns vary in function with current changes, and different diving patterns may be required, even if the point of entry is the same. Wrecks must also be approached using varying diving patterns, on the basis of the current. Normally, there are no buoys attached to wrecks in open water and anchoring over wrecks is undertaken using local land bearings or ultrasound equipment, adapting the approach to suit the particular conditions prevailing at each dive. Even when GPS positioning is used to approach a wreck, the approach must be adapted to take into account prevailing current and tidal conditions.
According to Norwegian law, lobster fishing is strictly prohibited in these waters, and no matter how tempting they

DIVING IN SWEDEN.

Diving along Sweden's elongated coasts is an adventure. While many foreign divers from warmer climates may balk at the thought of the cold murky Baltic waters, there is infinitely more to Swedish diving than just that, such as the chance to dive in two totally different ecological areas, for instance.
To the East, there is the Baltic Sea. A vast sea with brackish waters due to the many sweet water rapids flowing down the snowy mountains, through the country and out into the sea. On top of this, the shore area is covered with ice during the winter, making it appear dark and forbidding to marine plant and animal life, alike, to say nothing of divers who have to make do with reduced visibility. Divers often come across a few perches, bullheads or flat-fish - but the divers who come here don't have marine

stormy ocean. Visibility is often 25-30 meters in a landscape featuring sandy seabed, many drop offs, caves and ravines. There are a few wrecks, but the dive spots are dominated by marine life typical of the West coast: crabs, lobster, starfish, anemones, jelly-fish, anglerfish and catfish among others. Diving in the West coast is almost like diving in Norway and the further north you go, the better the diving. Air and water temperatures are low and visibility can be bad. In the summer, the water can reach 18-20 degrees close to the surface, but it is still cold further underwater. Most Swedish divers use dry suits all year round and lighting equipment is essential. Ice diving is a popular adventure during the long winter months, as well as stream diving in the typical Swedish rapids.

C

D

A - The sea anemone (Tealia felina) comes in a variety of colours, from drab olive green to bright purple red. Its tentacles are usually extended only at night.

B - In Swedish waters some species of shark can be found. The most common is the rather modest dogfish, (Squalus acanthias), that has a sharp spine in the dorsal fin.

C - The scallop clam (Pecten maximus) is usually encountered on deep sand or shingle seabeds. Its mortal enemy is the Arctic starfish Marthasterias glacialis, that can be seen here in the upper right hand corner.

D - Gobies are common, but the Atlantic spotted goby (Thorogobius ephippiatus) is a new arrival in Swedish waters where it was unknown until the 1980s. It usually lives in narrow cracks and crevices.

NARVIK Text by Nils Aukan

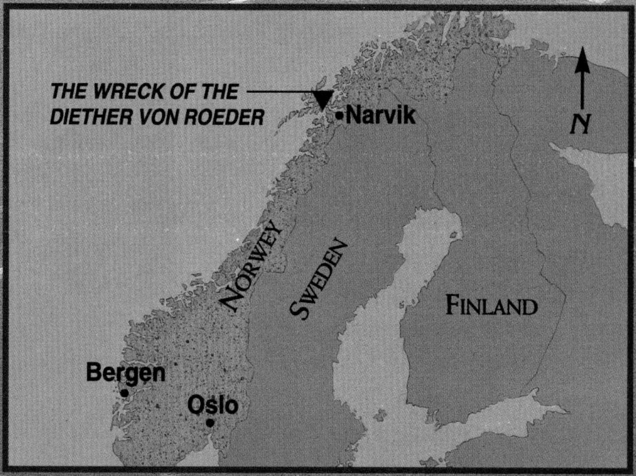

THE WRECK OF THE DIETHER VON ROEDER

Narvik

NORWEY
SWEDEN
FINLAND

Bergen

Oslo

N

12 m

20 m

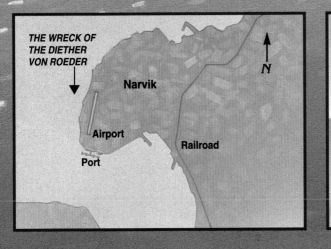

THE WRECK OF THE DIETHER VON ROEDER

Narvik

Airport

Port

Railroad

N

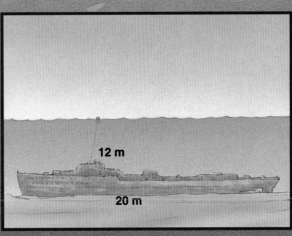

12 m

20 m

N arvik is famous for the wrecks lying in the port and in the fjords around the city. There are about 20 wrecks scattered around the harbour, all sunk between April 9th and 13th, 1940. On the night of April 9th, 1940, Norway was attacked by 10 German destroyers that sank two Norwegian warships, the *Norge* and the *Eidsvold*. Today, the *Norge* still lies in the harbour serving as a war grave. No diving is permitted on the *Norge*. Most of the *Eidsvold* was salvaged. All 10 German destroyers were sunk in a fierce sea battle with English destroyers between April 10th and 13th. The British lost two destroyers on April 10th, the *Hardy* and the *Hunter*. During those gun and torpedo battles, a large number of cargo ships waiting for iron ore were sunk in the harbour. During the British attack on April 10th, 1940,

the *Diether von Roeder*, moored to a pier in the harbour, was heavily damaged by 5 heavy 12 cm grenade shells from the British destroyer *Hardy*. The *Hardy* also launched its torpedoes, but they missed the destroyer, instead hitting and sinking one Swedish and one German cargo ship. On April 13th, the British warship *Warspite* attacked together with nine destroyers. The remaining German destroyers were sunk in various

locations in near-by fjords. The last was the *Diether von Roeder*. The British destroyer *Forester* slowly closed in on the doomed destroyer, unaware that the Germans had abandoned the ship after having set two depth bombs to go off nine minutes later. The Germans had intended the charges to go off when the British vessel was close enough to be caught in the resulting explosion but a land-based German

20 *Narvik*

D

E

machine gun opened fire from the shore too early and the British destroyer retreated. The charges went off, sinking the *Diether von Roeder* without damage to the British destroyer. To clear the harbour, the wreck, together with others, was later moved to Framnesodden. The destroyer *Diether von Roeder* Z-17 rests close to the remains of the destroyer *Anton Schmitt* Z-22 , at a depth of between 10 and 20 metres. The third destroyer *Anton Schmidt* Z-22,is lies on her side, not far from the other two wrecks.

All three wrecks can be visited in a single dive. Diving is possible all year round, but visibility is best during the fall, winter and early spring, when it can extend up to 30 metres. In the summer, visibility is still acceptable, at between 5 and 10 metres. This is purely a boat dive and the boat must be anchored in the correct position above the wrecks. There is an anchor buoy between the *Wilhelm Heidkamp* and the *Diether von Roeder*. The damage caused by the depth charges and the torpedoes, as well as the stripping operations undertaken by salvage companies, have greatly affected the look of the ships. Still, there are large sections to be explored. The bow is still intact. On the forward deck, that once housed the anchor, there is a huge hole, providing access to the inside of the wreck.

The armour of turret A is still in place although the barrel of the gun is missing. Turret B and the bridge were destroyed in the explosion.

A - Diving alongisde a German destroyer, overgrown by kelp.

B - A killer whale chases herring in the fjords off the coast between Narvik and Lofoten in the late fall.

C - Inside the German destroyer Diether von Roeder sunk by British destroyers on April 13, 1940.

Compartments and cabins are still intact but divers are ill-advised to venture into the wreck without a guideline that will lead them back safely. One can go into the wreck through certain open doors and take photographs. The stern stump has broken away and can be seen closer inshore at a depth of five metres, together with two bow pieces of the *Anton Schmitt*. In general, the current is rather weak. Exhausted air bubbles tend to disturb the silt, reducing visibility. Although most of the guns and munitions have been removed, certain unexploded munitions may still lie inside the wreck and must not be disturbed. The wrecks are overgrown by kelp that hangs in garlands and various species of yellow and orange sponges, alyconnarians and sea anemones especially Dahlia anemones and plumose anemones (*Metridium senile*). These wrecks abound in large spider crabs, sea urchins and starfish. Coalfish and pollack swim around freely while seawolves hide in the wrecks. Sunlight is scarce and lighting conditions are generally difficult, although visibility is nearly always sufficient. It is best to use ASA 200 film, with one or two powerful flashes. The site also offers opportunities for close-ups and macrophotography, using ASA 50 or ASA 100 film. The local diving centre and clubs organise visits to these wrecks.

D - Rockfish (Sebastes vivipares), are common on wrecks and rocks. They are generally found in small schools.

E - Ling (Molva molva), normally hovers alongside stones and crevices, but can also be found hiding in wrecks.

F - Thorny spider crabs (Lithodes maja) can be found crawling over wrecks and rocks. The can reach a size of 40-50 cm from leg to leg. They are found at depths greater than ten metres.

G - Starfish, purple sun stars (Solaster endeca), can be found everywhere.

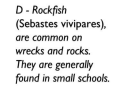

F

G

KRISTIANSUND Text by Nils Aukan

Mole of
Sørsundet

0 m

15 m

25 m

The city is surrounded by good diving sites. The town borders a fjord and the open Atlantic ocean. There are plenty of diving sites featuring wall-dives, drop-offs, soft corals, flat sand bottoms, rocks and kelp forests. Schooling fish such as coalfish, pollack and cod are common in areas where the current is strong. Diving can be done from a boat or directly from the shore, not far from parking lots.

The harbour, that is easily accessed by car, offers opportunities for good dives at depths varying between 15 to 25 metres, especially on the rock mole, Sørsundet, that lies at the south west entrance of the harbour. The large stone structure was built at the beginning of the 20th century, as a wave-breaker against waves from the south west. The top of the mole is paved with cement and there is a lighthouse at its tip. You can get into the water either by climbing down the rocks or walking along the pontoons of the boat harbour on the inside. Using a diving surface marker to indicate your presence as there is generally quite a lot of boating around the site. When surfacing, stay close to the kelp at the surface. You can get into the water at various spots and choose from a variety of diving patterns. To the east, close to the mole, you will find the four pillars of the bridge crossing the sound. Underwater, these pillars are covered by kelp and algae that are home to starfish, sea urchins and soft corals.

These waters are also frequented by schooling fish. The underwater life on and around the mole is fantastic. The gentle current attracts schools of fish around the tip of the mole. Seawolves (*Anarhicas lupus*) are found close to the rocks or lying on the open sand. This species normally feed on sea-urchins or crabs. Although it may seem ugly and threatening with its strong teeth and jaws, it is normally friendly. It can grow to impressive sizes, topping the scales

at 12-15 kg. The largest specimens weigh in at 20 kg. When disturbed, seawolves will raise their pectoral fins and extend their dorsal fin, in an attempt to intimidate intruders. Rockfish (*Sebastes viviparus*) hover close to the rocks near the tip of the mole at 15-22 metres below the surface. This inquisitive schooling species allows divers to approach and get quite close. They sometimes lie directly on the rocks, resting on their pectoral fins. Several ling (*Molva molva*), can be seen on each dive. Although generally a deep-water species, it comes to within 10 m of the surface in the summer. The larger specimens are between 1 and 1.5 metres in length. They keep close to the rocks, ready to disappear into nooks and cracks when divers approach. They, too, are inquisitive and poke their heads from between the rocks to observe the intruder. Schools of coalfish, (*Pollachius virens*), pollack (*Pollachius pollachius*) and cod (*Gadus morhua*) are common here, cruising back and forth in the gentle current. Anglerfish, (*Lophius piscatorius*) are also common and are usually encountered

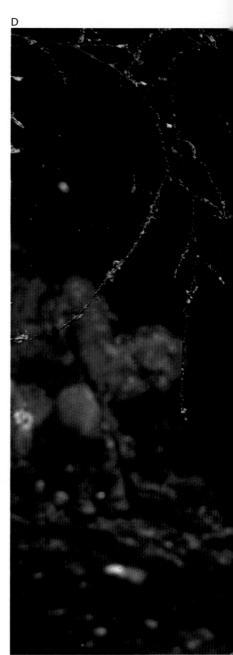

on each dive, resting on a rock or the sand bottom, using their camouflage to blend into their surroundings. These fish can come in all sizes with large specimes of up to 25 kg in these waters, although the species is known to grow to up to 50 kg.

Poor cod (*Trisopterus minutus*) is abundant in small schools. Dragonets (*Callionymus lyra*) as well as flatfish such as plaice (*Pleuronectes platessa*) can be seen on the sandy bottom, while the rocks are home to the small flatfish, Phrynorhombus norvegicus and Zeugopterus punctatus.

The shallows feature various kinds of kelp that provide shelter for a wide range of wrasses. The Ballan wrasse (*Labrus bergylta*) that comes in a variety of colours, is the largest. Colourful cuckoo-wrasses, (*Labrus bimaculatus*) are abundant. The small goldsinny,

(*Ctenolabrus rupestris*) can be seen everywhere, swimming in couples. The leopard-spotted goby (*Thorogobius ephippiatus*) lurks between rocks in the more sheltered areas of the mole. Butterfish (*Pholis gunnellus*) are also common, between the rocks and kelp. In both spring and autumn you will come across male lumpsuckers (*Cyclopterus lumpus*) guarding their eggs in a crevice.

Different sea-anemones of Tealia sp. are scattered on the rocks, together with some Metridium senile.

Edible crabs (*Cancer pagurus*) are common and you will also find a few large lobsters (*Homarus gammarus*) hiding under the rocks. Now and then, you will come across a large thorny spider crab (*Lithodes maja*).

Squat lobsters, especially the galathea strigosa, are plentiful and the anemone hermit crab (*Epagurus prideauxi*) can be found everywhere on the sandy bottom.Small nudibranches of various species are encountered on every dive, providing colourful subjects for macro-photographers. Limacia clavigera, polychera quadrilineata, Archidoris sp. are abundant and you will see Flabellina sp. feeding on tubularia hydroids. Aplysia punctata is also common.

The mole is also home to sea squirts, including the largest of the genus, the Ciona intestinalis, that can be found in clusters on kelp. The botryllus schlosseri comes in beautiful brown and yellow mats on kelp blades.

E

A - Large anemones (Bolocera sp.) *provide shelter for a thorny spider crab.*

B - *A soft coral, grows at the tip of the mole at 20 metres underwater.*

C - Anglerfish (Lophius piscatorius) *can be seen in small sizes, up to 20-30 kg of weight.*

D - *Rockfish,* (Sebastes vivipares) *are common on the point of the mole, resting on the rocks or hanging motionless in the gentle current.*

E - *Large Bolocera anemone with diver at the edge of the mole.*

VEVANGSTRØMMEN Text by Nils Aukan

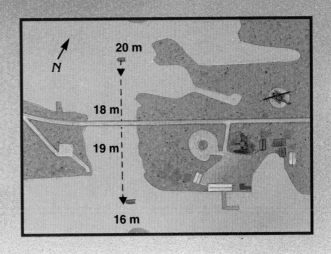

A - Soft coral and kelp
swaying in the Vevang
current.

B - Large stems in the
laminaria kelp forest.

C - Large Sea-wolf
resting at the bottom
with a diver closing in.
It is harmless if not
harassed or attacked.

Diving is possible in all seasons along the Atlanterhavsveien state highway that hugs the Atlantic coastline, near Strømsholmen, about 20 km to the south of Kristiansund. At the canal known as Vevangstrømmen (named after the nearby village of Vevang), the road turns eastwards for almost a mile through islands and reefs, banks and bridges. Divers can go into the water quite easily from the parking lots that flank the road. Diving in the Vevangstrømmen, features a very popular drift-dive in the strong current through a channel of beautiful orange and yellow soft-coral. It is relaxing to just float and watch the landscape as you drift along. You could also choose to dive slowly in slack current or during tidal changes. There are many different approaches to this dive. You can dive from outside towards the inside or vice versa. Diving depth is between 10 and 20 metres. If you extend the dive to the outside of the channel the depth may go down to 25 metres. Access to the dive spot is either by boat or by land. The current runs over a mainly rocky bottom, as in a canyon, and there are no dangerous outsprings. You should start the dive slowly. In the middle, it gets rather narrow and you are swept away at a thrilling speed through schools of coalfish and pollack. The bottom and both sides of the channel are covered with yellow and orange soft corals. If you feel that the current is too fast for your taste, you can always re-surface and abort the dive safely. The current reaches 5 to 6 knots at the most, but generally the speed is 2 to 4 knots. Close to the current you will encounter most of the fish species found in Norway. Schools of coalfish may suddenly block out the sunlight above you, while large pollacks lurk under them. Cod, especially, juveniles are very

B

common. Butterfish (*Pholis gunnelus*) and scorpionfish (*Myxocephalus scorpius*) hide amongst the soft coral. Seawolves, both juveniles and bluish grown-ups, are seen frequently as well as anglerfish. Various kinds of blennies take shelter amongst the rocks. You will also find various rays, such as the Raja clavata and the Raja radiata in these waters.
The current is flanked by seaweed, especially long Halydris siliquosa that grows up to 2 metres in length. Marine life in the algae belt is rather different from that found in the current. Amongst the seaweed, you will find needlefish such as Syngnathus acus and Entelurus aeqorus, growing up to 50 cm long. They remain immobile or swim very slowly, trusting their camouflage. The fifteen-spined stickleback (*Spinachia spinachia*) is very friendly and easy to approach.
If you watch the sponges closely, you will see the small caprella linearis that grows up to 4 cm, standing up on its hind feet and capturing tiny plancton with its claws. The lumpsucker (*cyclopterus lumpus*) also thrives on the sides of the current. Amongst the soft coral alcyonnarians, you find the large nudibranch Tritonia hombergi, that can attain a length of up to 20 cm. This nudibranch feeds on soft coral on which it also lays its pink egg-bands. Soft coral is also home to the small Midget-shrimp (*Eualus pusiolus*). At the sides of the current, towards the inside, there is plenty of kelp, Laminaria saccarina, laminaria digitata and saccaorhiza polychides. On the outside you will find more or less the same species together with the biggest variety of kelp, the Laminaria hyperborea, that can grow

D - Anglerfish
(Lophius piscatorius)
are common both on
sandy and rocky
bottoms.

E - Small juvenile sea-
wolf with it's brown
camouflage pattern.

A

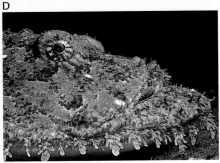

D

E

to a length of up to 3 - 4 meters. All kinds of algae, hydroids, sponges, sea-squirts and small crustaceans grow on the kelp stems. Starfish and sea-urchins feed between the kelp. In the crevices there are colourful anemones, especially the Urtecina fellina. Small Sagartia elegans can be seen between the soft corals. Night dives in the Vevanstrømmen reveal a very different sort of marine life. Access to the current edge is easy and navigation is further facilitated by the strong light. You will encounter the smallest squid, the 10-armed Sepiola

atlantica which comes out to hunt for small shrimps on the sandy bottom. The 8-armed octopus Eledone cirrhosa can also be seen hunting for crabs. Lobsters are encountered frequently and squat-lobsters such as the Galathea strigosa and Galathea squamifera come out from their dens. The crab Liocarcinus depurator crawls on the bottom, and the disguised macropodia rostrata can be seen hanging from the kelp.
The shrimp species Palaemon elegans and Pandalus montagui are frequently seen between the rocks, since they too

have nocturnal habits. Crangon crangon can be seen hiding in the sand, but is difficult to spot unless it moves.
The shy eelpout, (Viviparus blennius) rests amongst the sea-weed. You can also approach eels (Anguila anguila) up close in a way that is simply not possible during the day. The gurnard, (Eutrigla gurnardus) is seen walking on the bottom on its walking fins. Scorpionfish are everywhere, in a wild assortment of colours.
Even the shy Leopard-spotted Goby (Thorogobius aphippiatus), comes out from its hiding place under the ledges and can be caught on film using a 105 mm macro-lens. Most creatures are easy to watch during a night dive. The wrasses go to sleep, but you may be lucky enough to find them hiding in crevices, under a rock, or between the kelp.
Cod (Gadus morhua) can also be found sleeping amongst the kelp or on the open bottom during the night - an impressive sight.

AALESUND Text by Nils Aukan

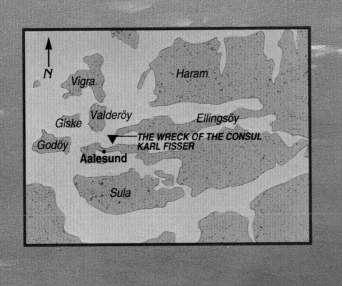

N

Vigra

Haram

Giske

Valderöy

Ellingsöy

THE WRECK OF THE CONSUL
KARL FISSER

Godöy

Aalesund

Sula

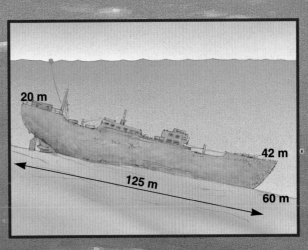

20 m

42 m

125 m

60 m

There are two diving centres in the city that organise diving trips. The centres specialise in underwater visits to the wrecks lying the port area where several World War II cargo steamers were sunk. One such vessel was the *Consul Karl Fisser*, bombed and sunk by six British Hudson aircraft on Sunday, May 3, 1942. An attempt was made to raise the ship after the war. The hawsers to the pontoons broke during raising operations and after just a few minutes above the surface, she sank once again to rest forever.

The wreck of the *Consul Karl Fisser* features a diving-depth of 20 meters from the surface to the top of the stern and 42 meters from the surface to the top of the bow. (The bow extends into deeper waters, up to 60 m, but dives at

depths greater than 30 m are not advisable in front of the bridge.) Because of the sheer size of the wreck, a full visit of the vessel requires two or three dives.

Diving should be undertaken from a boat with a guide who is familiar with the wreck that is located in open water in the fjord, at 10 minutes by boat from the Aalesund harbour. You can anchor

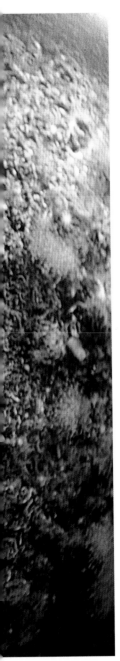

D

using GPS, cross-bearings from land, or ultrasound scanner. It is best to anchor at the stern section of the wreck. A good guide will have no trouble casting anchor close to the stern.

Once in the water at this point, explore the stern. The enormous rudder is still in place but the propeller has been recovered. Following the inside of the railing on one side, you can see the after-mast, still standing and still bearing a fishing net, now overgrown with algae and other marine life. The stern steering compartment is in place, its wooden roof partially devoured by teredo-worms. The reserve wheel inside the compartment has disintegrated.

The davits are swung out, since lifeboats were lowered while the vessel sank. The midship-area is vast and takes time to explore. Do not penetrate too deep into the wreck since your air bubbles will disturb silt and ruin visibility in seconds. This area is quite intact and very interesting to explore. A trip from the stern to the midship-area is quite enough on the first dive. Turn back at this point and swim along the other side of the wreck to get back to the stern. Follow the anchor line to the surface, ascending carefully. Make a safety stop at 3 metres.

An alternative approach is to start the dive at the midship area, then visit the stern, swimming back to the midship area to get to the surface vessel. The area in front of the bridge lies at a greater depth, making the dive shorter. This area mostly features empty holds.

A - The rear wheel-house is also overgrown with algae, and hydroids. The spare wheel can be seen to the left, without its wooden spikes. A diver and a thorny spider crab can be seen in the background.

B - Under the stern of "Konsul Karl Fisser". Large colonies of soft coral, anemones and Metridium senile.

This wreck makes an excellent subject for photographers. Visibility is generally quite good, between 10 to 20 metres. In the winter, visibility can even reach 30 or 40 metres, but the lighting may not be as good. Close to the surface, visibility can be as low as 5 metres in the summer, but improves at depths greater than 10 metres.

The stern is beautifully carpeted with hundreds of Dahlia anemones and Metridium senile. The railing, still standing around the stern is overgrown with sponges, soft coral alcyons and hydroids. Nudibranches are also common between the hydroids and soft coral. Kelp does not grow at this depth. There are hundreds of large sea squirts (Ciona intestinalis) in the net hanging from the after mast. Schooling fish such are large yellow pollack and coalfish swim around the wreck. Large blue wolffish (Anarbicas lupus) are often seen inside the wreck. Schools of coalfish and pollack cruise between the masts, deck accommodations and davits. Spider crab and large brown sea cucumber abound. This wreck also features an abundance of large edible crabs (Cancer pagurus).

C - Large jelly-fish (Cyanea capillata) must be handled with care. Some can be really big, and lots of young fishes hide between the burning stings.

D - The wreck railing is completely overgrown with hydroids and soft coral.

E - Anglerfish (Lophius piscatorius) has a special camouflage-pattern on its jaw, blending against the bottom.

F - Close-up of the head of a plaice.

E

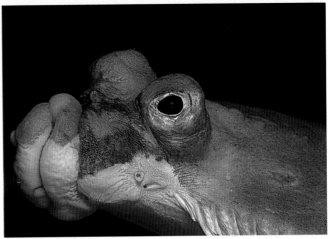
F

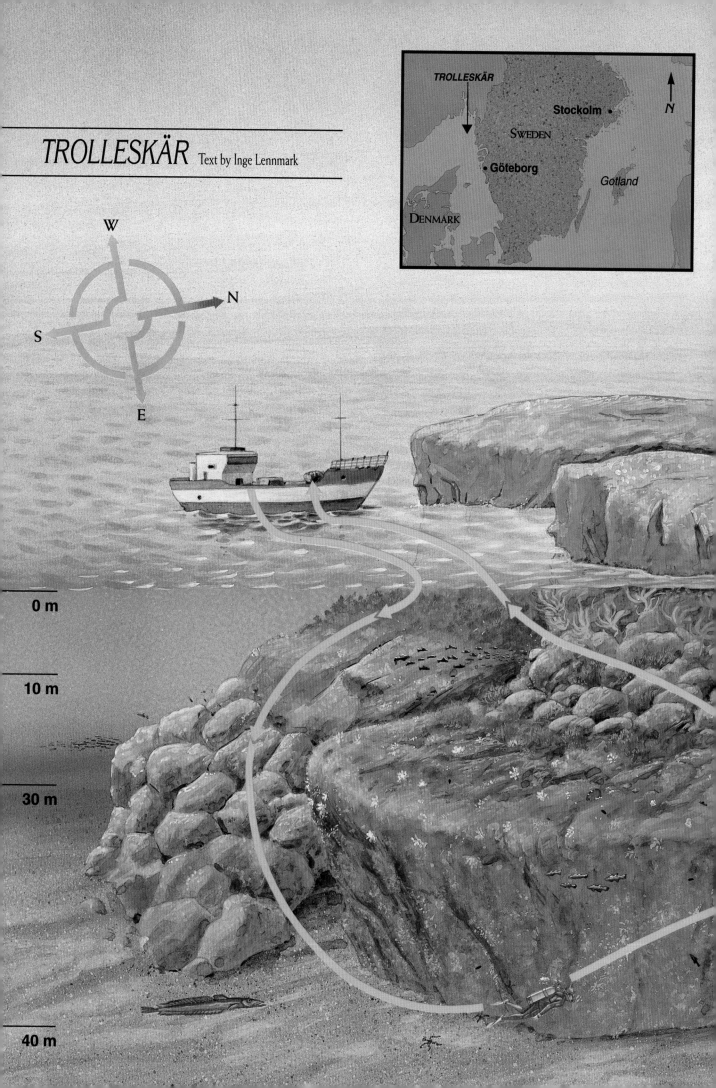

TROLLESKÄR Text by Inge Lennmark

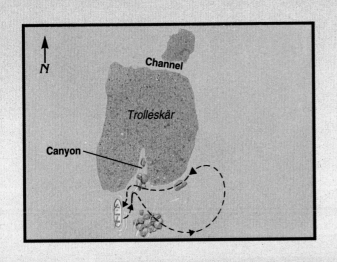

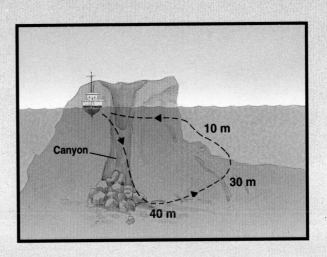

A

iving in the Väderö archipelago
while staying on the mainland
means a lot of boat riding and
limited time for diving. One alternative is
to join a diving cruise ship with live-aboard
facilities. It is best to moor near to the
steep southern face of Trolleskär, on one
of the few calm days in the late summer.
Diving can be undertaken here on just a
few days each season, since Trolleskär is
exposed to the fury of the winds and the
waves from all directions. Why go through
the trouble of going there in first place?
Well, first of all, visibility is excellent
when compared to more inshore waters.
Secondly, the bottom is cleaner – less
covered with silt and sediment, because of
the waves and strong current. Thirdly, this
is an ideal location to catch a glimpse of
some exclusive Atlantic salinity-loving
species, that disdain the brackish surface
waters closer to the mainland. The
closest land mass is the coast of England.
Divers ought to submerge from the ship
and take a short surface swim towards the
canyon. You cannot fail to notice the
bluish green hue of water, so different
from the yellowish green closer to the
mainland coast. The bottom between the
surface and the kelp forest is also
different. Instead of green tuft algae
interspersed by bladderwrack plants, the
rocks here are covered by countless
common mussels (Mytilus edulis), that
attract a similar crowd of hungry starfish
(Asterias rubens). At the bottom of the
canyon you will see a heap of rounded
granite boulders piled one on top of the
other. Use your torch to peer between
boulders and perhaps catch a glimpse of a

B

A - Kelp forests are
some of the richest
biotopes of the world,
and are often
compared with coral
reefs and rain forests.
Here are some plants
of Laminaria digitata
on the edge of a rock
ledge.

B - Dead man's finger
(Alcyonium
digitatum) is the
dominant coral species
at depths between 10
and 25 metres. Mostly
the colonies are just
one "finger", but some
may reach impressive
size.

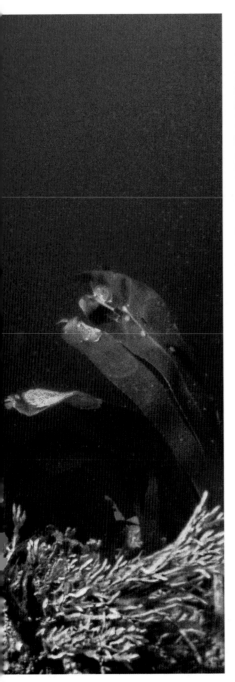

C

giant Maine lobster (*Homarus gammarus*) or a ferocious-looking sea wolf (*Anarhichas lupus*). If you are very lucky indeed, you may even come across sharks in the open water. It is the rather modest horned dogfish (*Squalus acanthias*) but sleek and elegant like other sharks nevertheless.

Around the corner of the plateau, east of the canyon wall, there is a steep cliff face that is actually a mountain wall forming a negative drop-off, with lots of cracks, crevices and small rock shelves. Along the wall, you will encounter some species of starfish, that are otherwise rare in Swedish waters: the red and white *Porania pulvillus*, the beige *Hippasterias phrygiana* and, on the white gravel below the cliff face, the sun-star *Solaster endeca*. Clinging to ledges, you will see a few

exquisite feather stars or crinoids (*Antedon petasus*) each in individual bright colours ranging from brilliant yellow over cream to a deep purple red. Their presence here indicates periodic strong currents. Reaching the top of the wall, you enter the realm of dead man's fingers (*Alcyonium digitatum*), on a wide plateau at a depth between 20 and 30 m. White sea urchins (*Echinus acutus*) are strewn over the landscape. A lemon dab (*Microstomus kitt*) poses in front of the camera, utterly confident that its camouflage makes it totally invisible. The colours of the dab perfectly imitate the pale pink calcareous algae and splotches of orange sponges in the surroundings. A ling (*Molva molva*) hurries by. You unexpectedly encounter an absolutely marvellous cuckoo wrasse (*Labrus bimaculatus*) in his speckled shining metal blue costume, a male defending his territory. His flashing white forehead announces his determination to chase away any intruder, regardless of size or species. As you look back over the edge of the precipice, a ballan wrasse stands guard among edible sea urchins (*Echinus esculentus*) against the backdrop of a school of pollack (*Pollachius pollachius*). Laminarians grow high in the kelp forest, at depths from 10 to 20 meters. This is a good place to look for nudibranches. Some kelp leaves are covered with bryozoans (genuses *Electra* and *Membranipora*). You may also find the minuscule *Limacia clavigerina* here. On the bottom, among the red calcareous algae, the steel-blue *Aeolidia papillosa* hunts for

hydrozoans and other small cnidarians. The highlight of this unique diving spot is - a cave. Caves in Scandinavian bedrock are almost a geological impossibility. At this spot however, at a depth of 17 metres, a heap of boulders seem to have piled on to a huge granite block, so as to form a cave between the boulders and the rock face. The walls and ceilings of the cave are carpeted with yellow sponges. In one of the openings, a strangely shaped sponge (*Axinella verrucosa*) hangs like a chandelier. The cave floor features a number of Jago's goldsinnies (*Ctenolabrus rupestris*) in very peculiar colours. Their relatives in the kelp forest are dark olive green and purple, but these cave dwellers wear pale shades varying from yellow over cream to pink – clearly mimicking the hues of their habitat. The last leg of the dive involves crossing the canyon to get back aboard the Conatus. After a hot sauna and magnificent dinner. What could be more tempting than a night dive? It may be a good idea to take the Zodiac to the northern side. Small squid have been spotted at night, in the shallow channel between Trolleskär and the next islet.

D

C - After severe winters featuring thick ice cover, rocks in shallow areas are colonised by the common mussel (Mytilus edulis). The mussels will soon be attacked by an army of starfish (Asterias rubens).

D - Flatfish are masters of camouflage. This lemon dab (Microstomus kitt) believes itself to be invisible and appears to be posing for the camera, while perfectly imitatating the colours of its surroundings.

STENSKÄR Text by Inge Lennmark

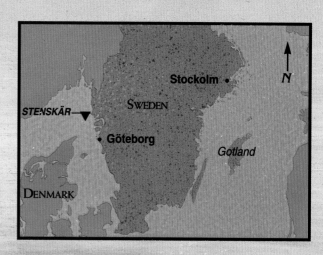

STENSKÄR

Stockolm

SWEDEN

Göteborg

Gotland

DENMARK

N

W

N

S

E

0 m

30 m

40 m

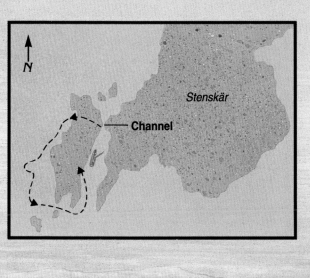

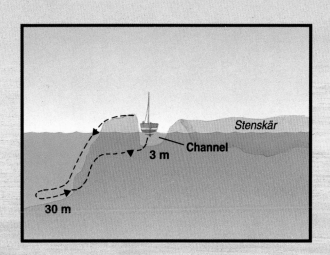

Easily accessible within half an hour by boat from a number of dive centres in the area, Stenskär has a lot to offer both SCUBA divers and snorkelers. The dive boat enters a sheltered bay and is moored to a natural shelf among the smooth rocks onshore. All SCUBA equipment is unloaded and carried across a narrow rock ledge to the western part of the island, where the divers don their gear. Snorkelers and swimmers should follow the narrow channel between the two parts of the island and start exploring the lagoon just north of it. The SCUBA divers should follow the steep western slope downwards. Tufts of green algae cover the rocks between the bladderwrack plants (*Fucus vesiculosus*) down to a couple of meters below the surface. Dense schools of

A

millions of small gobies (*Coryphopterus flavescens*) glitter in the sun as they flit about amongst the bladderwrack. At a depth of about 5 m, you ought to reach a kelp forest featuring large leaves of laminarians (mostly *Laminaria digitata*) swaying the water. Push the foliage apart and peer down to see what is hidden underneath, on the bottom between the stems. Chances are, you will see inquisitive and colourful wrasses, mostly Jago's goldsinny (*Ctenolabrus rupestris*) and pipefishes (family *Syngnathidae*) among sea anemones (*Tealia felina*) on rocks covered by green sponges and calcareous red algae (genus *Lithothamnion*).

On the way down, you should gives this area only a cursory exploration since there will be plenty of time to study it in detail on the way back, as you rise towards the surface following the southern contour of the island.

B

Below the kelp forest, at a depth of about 15 m, you will come across a field of red algae. From this point onwards, a hands-off approach is required, together with careful buoyancy control. An underwater torch is very useful, even in broad daylight. Sunlight penetrating at this depth is green, so you will need the white light of the torch to be able to appreciate the bright colours of the underwater world. Peer into cracks and crevices, to try to get a glimpse of the black gobies (*Gobius niger*) and leopard-spotted gobies (*Thorogobius ephippiatus*) that lurk there. The torch will reveal the splendid purple of the *Dilsea* algae that appear jet black in the natural green light from the surface.

We have reached the twilight zone of sessile animals, dominated by the leathery coral dead man's fingers (*Alcyonium digitatum*). An abundance of colourful bottom-dwellers share this habitat with

C

A - An awful nuisance when the stinging tentacles touch naked skin, the red jellyfish (Cyanea capillata) is nevertheless a real beauty when encountered in shallow water.

B - Pipefishes are closely related to sea horses. They live amongst seaweed or in

eelgrass meadows. This orange species is an Entelurus aequorus.

C - However tempting it may be to pick an edible crab (Cancer pagurus), this is strictly forbidden in Sweden. The penalty can be confiscation of boat and diving equipment.

(*Stenogorgia rosea*) and even a small solitary calcareous madreporarian coral (*Caryophyllia smithii*). But most gorgonian specimens are just single strands, and the madreporarians are no bigger than a width of a thumb.

This dive moreover does give you a change to see some extremely fascinating soft-bottom dwellers.

Coarse sand made of bits and pieces from seashells covers the bottom close to the wall. You will soon come across a few clam mussels (*Pecten maximus*) and later, an Arctic starfish (*Marthasterias glacialis*). These two are mortal enemies. Provoke the clam shell by placing the starfish close to it, and the shell swims away, shells clattering, in a cloud of silt. Further out is a flat bottom of mud. At first it seems devoid of life. Finally, you will come across a sea pen (*Pennatula phosphorea*), and perhaps a few beautiful cerianthid sea anemones (genus *Cerianthus*) and sea cucumbers (genuses *Holothuria* and *Psolus*). Soon our diving computers urge us to turn around and ascend. To ascend you can go back the way you came, or ascend safely by following the wall up to a depth of 9 m and then swimming southwards, around the corner at the southern tip of the island, to then head north into the bay at a depth of about 3 m. On the last leg of the return trip, you can stop to admire whelks (*Buccinum undatum*) and shore crabs (*Carcinus maenas*), on the sandy bottom of the bay. The shore crabs in these waters, are strikingly more colourful than in bays closer to the mainland. Stenskär is an island that deserves more than one dive. You could go snorkeling in the lagoon, where you will encounter flatworms (*Prosthecereus vittatus*) and try to avoid the stinging tentacles of the beautiful red jellyfish (*Cyanea capillata*). When swimming northwards along the shore to see the eelgrass meadow, you may come across a pregnant male pipefish (*Entelurus aequorus*). Pregnant male? Oh yes. The female lays her eggs on the belly of the male, where he fertilises them, carries and nurtures them until they hatch.

D

D - Brittle stars (family Ophiuroidae) spend most of the day hiding. This hard-bottom species can be found under stones and in narrow fissures. They can generally be seen only by torchlight, even during the day.

E - The "lagoon", just North of the bay where we moored the dive boat, is only 2-3 m deep. The unusually luxuriant vegetation of algae and seaweed makes it an ideal place for snorkelling.

the coral: sea anemones of several species, sun starfish (*Crossaster papposus*), edible crabs (*Cancer pagurus*) and bristleworms of many kinds. The most dazzling one is the sessile peacock fan worm (*Sabella pavonina*), whose long tubes made of mucus and mud protrude up to 30 cm from the bottom. If we are extremely careful, we may even see the worm's wonderful fan of tentacles. Down here, the layer of sediments on the bottom is clearly disturbing. Careful movements and scrupulous buoyancy control are absolutely necessary.

So far, we have descended along a nearly vertical wall of solid rock. At 25 to 30 m we encounter large boulders at the foot of the precipice. Brittle stars (family *Ophiuroidae*) and squat lobsters (*Galathea strigosa*) striped in bright red and blue are hidden in the crevices. Sessile species include ascidians or sea squirts (*Ciona intestinalis*), red gorgonian coral

THE WRECK OF THE
SAPPEMEER Text by Ulrika Kroon

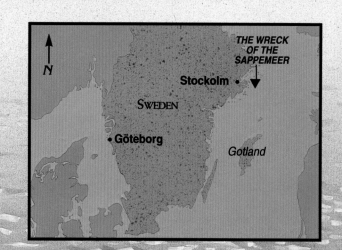

N

THE WRECK
OF THE
SAPPEMEER

Stockolm •

SWEDEN

• Göteborg

Gotland

0 m

15 m

25 m

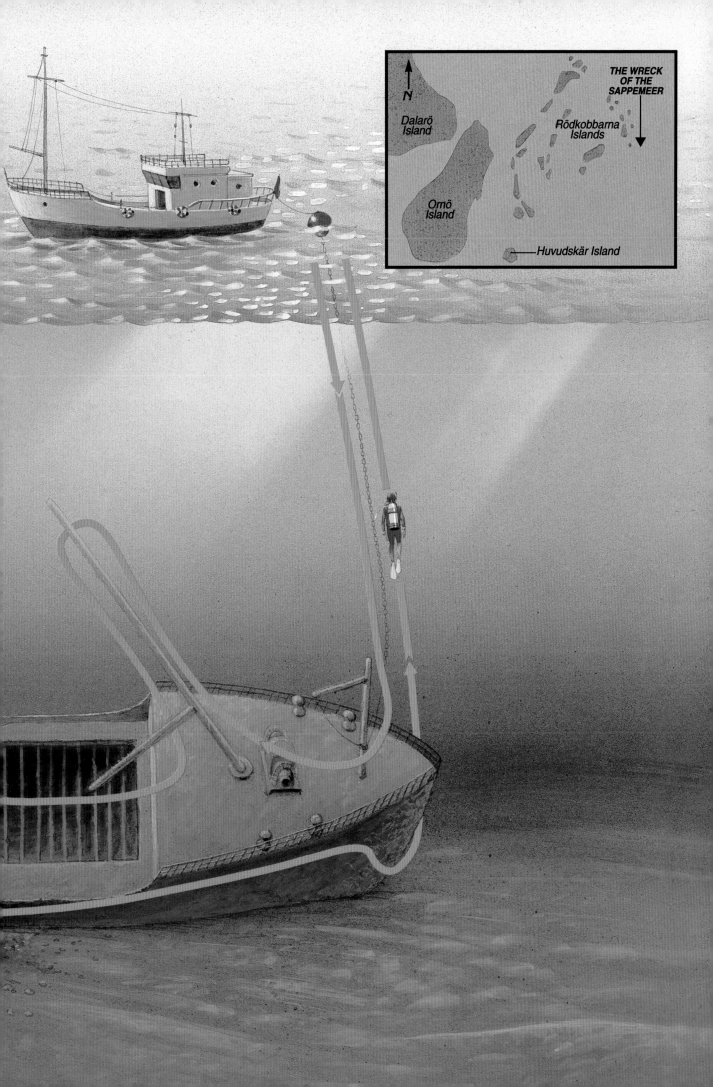

THE WRECK
OF THE
SAPPEMEER

N

Dalarö
Island

Örnö
Island

Rödkobbarna
Islands

Huvudskär Island

Since the 17th century, at least 10,000 vessels have sunk in the Baltic Sea, along the eastern coast of Sweden. No waters in the world, except perhaps the Great Lakes in the United States, have a similar amount of such well-preserved wrecks. The wrecks here are in excellent condition mainly because of the lack of tides and the brackish water, that prevents shipworm from destroying the remains of the sunken ships.

The southern parts of the Stockholm Archipelago are among the busiest shiplanes along the East coast, mainly because most of the ships headed for the capital have to pass through it. Today, both 20th century steel wrecks and wooden wrecks, hundreds of years old, are scattered in this area.

On the dark and stormy night of November 7th 1969, the steel freighter *Sappemeer* put out from the southern part of Sweden bound for Iggesund, further north in the Baltic Sea. The Swedish vessel that was built at Delfzijl in Holland in 1961, was carrying a cargo of 649 tons of shingle (coarse gravel). Faced with strong winds, her Master decided to use the more sheltered route, through the islands. After the crew retired for the night, the vessel was switched onto automatic steering. This proved to be a

B

big mistake. At 10.30 p.m. the crew was awakened by a terrifying noise. Probably because of the strong wind, the ship had veered off course and hit a skerry, sustaining severe damage to her bow. Her crew couldn't do much but send a distress signal in the hope of being rescued. The *Sappemeer* rapidly lost stability in the stormy conditions and just when the crew had decided to abandon the vessel in life boats, a

C

A

D

A - The impressive stem, emerging from the dark green water at a depth of 18 metres, is the sight that greets you when you reach the end of the tagline.

B - Divers peeking into the superstructure may swim through areas where the crew used to reside.

C - The first floor of the superstructure is still intact on the ship's port side. Down here, by the deck, divers can still peek through the small windows into the remains of the cabins and the machinery.

D - At the starboard side of the ship, the hull has sunken deep into the sea bed. The ladder, which formerly led down into the storage rooms, is now covered with shingle, like the seabed around the wreck.

E - There are many interesting details to look at, especially on the foredeck. A winch still stands, as well as this windlass and the two masts.

Swedish Air Force helicopter came to their rescue. The next morning, there was no trace of the ship. It was many months before the wreck was located. Today, the *Sappemeer* rests tilted 45 degrees on one side, reflecting the same instability as when she was sinking. The wreck is situated in the open sea, quite far from the busy archipelago, and is therefore rather exposed to windy weather. But if you are lucky, the sea can be calm as a mirror when you reach the spot.

There is a buoy on the surface, marking the position of the wreck. The buoy is also used to attach the dive boat and the tagline for the divers. Follow the chain, attached to the buoy. A few metres below the surface, it changes to a thick rope and at a depth of about 10 metres, you could begin to get a glimpse of the wreck below you. It is a beautiful sight, as she emerges in the green and sometimes very murky Swedish waters. When visibility is exceptionally good, almost half of the 51 meter long ship can be seen at the same time. The tagline is attached to the stem, which is situated at a depth of about 18 metres. The maximum depth at the bottom, which is flat and sandy, is 28 meters. At first sight, the wreck can seem rather confusing with the marked lop-sidedness to her starboard side and the sometimes bad visibility. If you are unfamiliar with this wreck or visibility is bad, use a reel. Otherwise you could end up in a cargo hold and get lost.

Beginning the dive on the foredeck, there are many interesting things to look at. A winch still stands there, as well as many bitts and the windlass. The two masts, of which one is situated on the foredeck, are intact and lean 45 degrees starboard, just like the ship. It looks strange, the way they peek out into nowhere. Wires can still be seen hanging from the masts. There is very little vegetation on the wreck. Except from some mussles, who have decided to take over the wreck, the ship is bare of sea weed and corals. It looks like she sank yesterday. Also, there is an absolute lack of fish. The *Sappemeer* is definitely a wreck only for wreck fanatics.

Following the port side, passing the masts and the cargo holds to your left, you eventually reach the superstructure. It has three floors. The top floor with the bridge and the funnel has no roof, making it easy to peek in. Crewmen's quarters were located on the second floor. It is quite easy to pass through doors and windows, if you have adequate training and experience. The last floor housed the engine room and a few cabins.

You have now reached the stern, the name *Sappemeer*, still clearly legible. The large rudder still stands in place. It is now time to go back and finish the dive. Following the starboard side, you reach the cargo holds. The wreck has sunk down on its side into the sea bed at a depth of 28 meters. The cargo of shingle has poured out from the open holds onto the sea bed. The large cargo holds are easy to enter, but there is nothing left in there but stones and the steel remains of the wreck. Following the starboard side to the stem, you can take a last look at the foredeck mast and peek into the hatches on the foredeck, before finding your way back to the tagline and up to the dive boat.

E

SOUTHERN BALTIC SEA AND NORTH SEA

NORVEGIAN
SEA

BALTIC
SEA

LILLE BELT

FEHMARN AND
THE WRECK
OF THE STEN TRANS

THE WRECK OF THE JAN HEWELIUSZ

OESTERDAM,
ZEELANDBRUNG AND
WEMELDINGE

A - Small is beautiful in the Baltic Sea. Young sea pink with outstretched tentacles protected by nettle capsules, on the wreck of the Brage.

B - In the clean shallows of the Baltic Sea, one also comes across sea slugs that favour clear water.

C - Anemone, oyster, synascidian. Typical underwater scenery in the Oosterschelde with a yellow sea-squirt (Ciona intestinalis).

D - Sea pink anchored to an edible mussel. This sort of growth on stable ground surfaces is typical of the western Baltic. Sea pink use their tentacles to capture plankton that they ingest through their gaping mouths. The water around wrecks that are frequently overgrown with sea pink, is significantly clearer than the surrounding water, since as they feed, sea pink also clean and filter the water.

The first time I went diving to visit a wreck in the Baltic sea, I felt a strong urge to resurface after the first five metres. It was bitterly cold and the anchor line, along which we were diving, disappeared just a few arm-lengths in front of my hand, into a blackish green darkness. Fortunately, I decided to dive on further with the others. I shall never forget the sight as 'our first Baltic wreck' appeared before our eyes in relatively clear waters, after we had passed through the layer of water rendered turbulent by the current. The sunken ship, a small cargo vessel seemed like a huge flower-basket that someone, acting on some marvellous whim, had placed on the sand under 18 metres of water. We only managed to identify this giant flower-basket as an old sailing ship, when on closer examination, we could distinguish the stock anchor on the bow. One must have an experienced eye to distinguish between the bow and the

E - Sea pink anchored by its suction foot on the hard back shell of a shore crab. Being constantly carried around, this sea pink is ensured plentiful food from the open water.

stern, the top and the bottom of such a wreck, and even then, in the case of very large wrecks several dives may be needed to do this - so great is the toll that underwater contact with the sea exacts from a ship. Despite the bitter cold, we remained in our wet suits underwater for three quarters of an hour and I used all the film in my camera. The pictures - and my camera hardly captured many close-ups during these first diving expeditions - surprised all those who saw them, myself included. As the reader may have guessed, the diving sites featured in the following pages almost exclusively feature wrecks. This is mainly because, in the total absence of reefs, wrecks become a sort of 'Oasis of Life' in the midst of a seemingly endless desert of water. Besides sand and slime, there is indeed little to see around wrecks in the Baltic. Since the water is filtered and suspended particles removed by the fixed underwater flora and fauna developing on wrecks, visibility falls sharply as soon as one moves a little way from a wreck. It must also be borne in mind that diving in the Baltic Sea off the German or Danish coast, or in the North Sea off the Dutch coast, is quite different from diving in the Mediterranean or in the Tropics. Diving in the Northern waters requires more equipment and safety precautions. At these diving sites, the air temperature alone rises significantly as summer approaches. The water temperature remains constant all the year round, which is to say, the sea is always very cold. A water temperature of 4°C in winter and 8°C in summer is to be

D

hood, is advisable even in summer, if one intends going out to sea on a diving base vessel - especially since divers easily fall prey to colds!

Protection from the cold is obviously even more important when diving. In the winter, a dry suit is most advisable. In summer one could venture into the water with only a semi-dry suit. Dry suits are recommended all the year round if deep and long wreck diving tours are envisaged. To prevent possible malfunctions, when using dry suits and when no further help is available, one ought also to use a life jacket or life vest. Not only the diver, but also diving equipment is subject to the problems caused by low temperatures! At water temperatures of about 4°C or lower, the breath regulator is at risk of freezing. The most common sign that this is

taking place is an uncontrolled air flow out of the affected regulator. All breath regulators used for visiting underwater wrecks in cold waters must be protected against freezing and icing, in keeping with the latest technology. Certain sites are exposed to very strong currents. This applies especially to diving sites located off the Dutch and Danish coasts, within the Little Belt. In these areas, all divers must consult local diving centres for precise information on tide timings, so as to go into the water only when tidal currents safely permit diving!

Diving is best undertaken in winter or spring when underwater visibility conditions are at their best. From January to March, underwater visibility in the Baltic Sea reaches 15 metres, while it extends up to 20 metres during the same period in the North Sea off the Dutch coast. While temperatures may be more inviting in the summer, the water is also infested by billions of plankton particles that multiply at an incredible rate, making the best of the warmer temperature and sunlight to form what divers call "bouquets of algae". This can result in zero underwater visibility for days on end. July and August are the months most affected by this phenomenon. Although the difficulties involved with diving at the sites described here demand a higher degree of skill than that required at other diving sites, the first encounter with a new, mysterious, wreck that is difficult to reach underwater, is still today one of the most fascinating experiences I have ever enjoyed. I sincerely hope that this will also apply to you!

C

expected at the usual diving depth of about 20 metres. A somewhat warmer temperature can only be expected during purely shallow water diving expeditions very close to the beach. But even in this case, the temperature hardly ever rises above 14°C. In this temperature range, protection against the cold is an imperative precaution, and must be worn both on the land and in the sea. A thick, weatherproof jacket, complete with

E

LILLE BELT Text by Carsten Werner

Faenö
Kalv

7 m

13 m

W

S

N

E

7 m

13 m

A

The waterway between the mainland of Jutland and the isle of Fyn is called the Lille Belt. This waterway is the smallest of three connections linking the Baltic Sea with the Kattegat. The other connections are called Store Belt and Öresund.

The Lille Belt is famous for its good diving conditions and attracts many divers especially from Jutland and the north of Germany, who can reach its shores easily by road.

Though it is possible to get into the water at almost any place on the coastline, the small island of Faenö Kalv in the middle of the Lille Belt is probably the best dive site in this area. The island is uninhabited.

Immediately upon getting into the water, divers realise that the rather rough boat ride to the island is well worth the trouble. The influx of fresh

B

nutrient-rich water attracts a wide variety of marine life, that is particularly abundant on the north-eastern coast of the island. Lumpsuckers, plaice, grey gurnards and butterfish are common. The wide range of smaller marine life is impressive and gives the underwater photographer good chances to fill many rolls of film with close-up shots. Colourful sponges and soft corals, anemones, different kinds of

C

nudibranchia, sea slugs and mussels, spider crabs and whelks make the time pass much too quickly under water.

Best diving conditions are in spring and autumn, though it can be quite cold at these times of the year and a semi-dry or better still, a dry-suit is recommended, especially during the boat ride to and from the island.

Currents have to be taken into account, since they vary and can be strong,

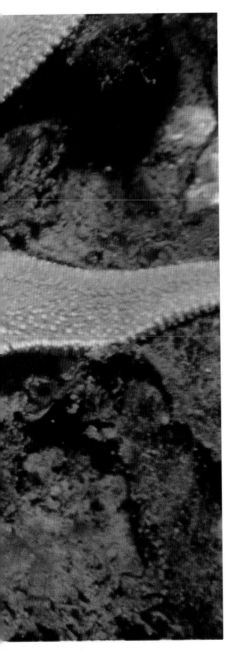

dives, the most diversified dives don't have to surpass 15 metres. The bottom mainly features sand, rocks and gravel. The above diving conditions imply that a diver should at least have some experience and beginners should be in company of an experienced diver. For these divers, time spent under water in the Lille Belt will be unforgettable and many divers return year after year. There are some more facts that make diving in the Baltic Sea, the two Belts and the Sund a unique experience. The Baltic Sea is a marginal sea on the continental shelf with an average depth of only 52 metres and a maximum depth of 452 metres in the vicinity of the island of Gotland. The area is 415,000 square kilometres and the volume - due to the shallow conditions - only 22,000 cubic kilometres.

Many rivers from Poland, Russia, Lithuania, Latvia, Estonia, Finland, Sweden, Denmark and Germany empty into the Baltic Sea. The catchment area covers 1.7 million square kilometres or 17% of Europe.

Only the three narrow straits providing access from Denmark allow water exchange with the open seas. As a result, it takes between 25 and 35 years for a complete water exchange of the Baltic Sea (compared to only 3 to 3.5 years in the North Sea). Due to the influx of many fresh water rivers there is a constant draining of surface water with a low salinity into the North Sea and a constant influx of highly saline deep sea water. The salinity in the western parts of the Baltic Sea reaches it's peak at about 15 parts per thousand, compared to only 3 parts per thousand in the east.

Vertical water exchange is very limited, causing temperature belts and salt layers that can surprise an inexperienced diver, causing sharp drops in temperature and visibility. This, however, is no reason for concern, since visibility usually improves with increased depth.

About 9% of the exchange water passes

through the Lille Belt. Tidal differences are negligible.

On the north coast of Faenö Sund there is a holiday centre that offers comfortable rental accommodation at reasonable prices: Middelfart FerieCenter, Oddevejen 8, 5500 Middelfart, Denmark, phone 0045-64 41 06 10. Rental accommodation is about 70 square metres with one living room with an open kitchen, two bedrooms and two bathrooms. They are suitable for up to 6 persons, and rent is about DM 1000.- for one week and DM 1600.- for two weeks. The village has a restaurant, a small shop, swimming pool and sauna.

For non-divers there are many places of interest on the mainland Jutland and the island of Fyn.

Divers dependent on a compressor can ask the management for advice - this should be done in advance and double-checked. There is a public slipway for small boats in the port of Middelfart.

A - Common starfish (Asterias rubens). The animal is shown pulling on a mussel's closed shell until it opens. It will then insert it's stomach into the mussel and dissolve and digest the living animal. Three common whelks (Buccinum undatum) are waiting for their own share of the meal.

B - Common mussels (Mytilus edulis) covered by several small common starfish.

C - Spawn of Drummond facelina (Facelina auriculata). The photo was taken in spring, when the animals reproduce.

D - Sugar kelp (Laminaria saccharina), with lots of common starfish on both sides.

E - Plumose anemone (Metridium senile). They have about 1000 tentacles that come in wide range of colours: pale white, brown, yellow and red.

especially during stormy weather. Currents do not necessarily follow the shipping channel, but can flow crossways once in a while. Very often there are counter-currents parallel to the shore. Usually the currents depend on the direction of the wind: winds from east and south to south-west cause currents to the north, winds from other directions normally cause currents to the south. Currents can change from day to day and there are many days without any current worth mentioning at all. For safety reasons the boat should stay manned permanently when divers are underwater, remaining alert to provide assistance in case of emergency. Maximum water depths in the Lille Belt reach more than 80 metres in some areas, but the shorelines offer abundant chances for interesting shallow dives. There is actually no reason to do deep

THE WRECK OF THE JAN HEWELIUSZ

Text by Stefan Baehr

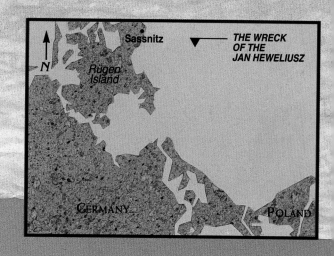

THE WRECK
OF THE
JAN HEWELIUSZ

Sassnitz

Rügen
Island

GERMANY

POLAND

N

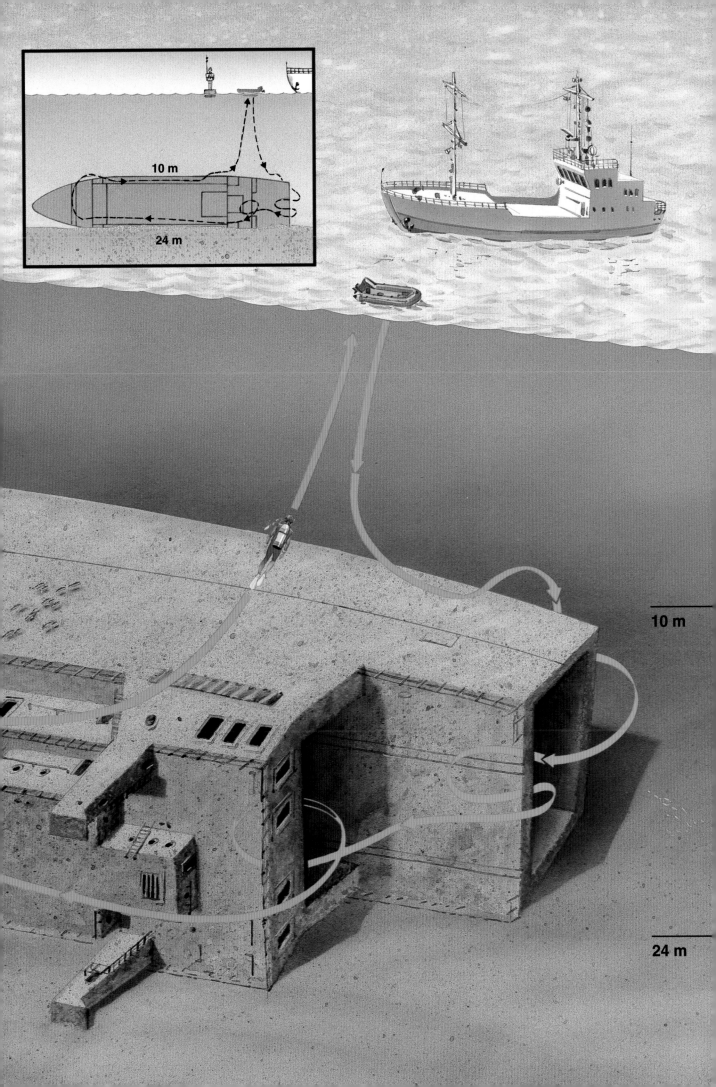

10 m

24 m

10 m

24 m

Facing seven metre high waves in the midst of the hurricane on 14.01.93 'Verena', the Polish ferry *Jan Heweliusz* capsized and sank. Shortly before the accident, the vessel had suffered sea-damage. As on many previous occasions, she had once again driven into a dock wall at Ystad in Sweden. According to the report by the engineer in charge of repairing the ship, she had suffered extensive damage to her stern bulwark. To quote his words, 'she simply wasn't going to make it'. The ship owners did their best to downplay the whole incident, in a bid to minimise wharfage costs. So it was decided to carry out repairs in phases. Whenever the ship was in Swinemünde, a little more welding work was undertaken. It was later found that out of a total of ten securing mechanisms of the stern ramp, five anchoring bolts were missing. They were either simply carried away or otherwise deprived of their function, because without them, the stern ramp could not be closed!

That fateful night 68 people were on board the *Jan Heweliusz* on. The ship's captain, Andrzej Ulasiewicz, was later found dead by Naval divers in full uniform in his cabin. It was obvious that he hadn't tried to save himself.

The last resting place of the Jan Heweliusz lies at about 15 nautical miles transversely from Sassnitz on the island of Rügen. The wreck's geographical co-ordinates are 54° 36′38″N 14° 13′10″E. The ship lies on her port side. With a 24-metre deep seabed, the wreck towers up to 10 metres below the surface. Since this poses a navigational hazard, the

wreck's position is signalled by a buoy. Unfortunately, like the entire bridge and the side walls of the upper vehicle deck, certain interesting details such as the davits were carried away.

Through the very large breach in the stern, one can swim into the ferry. If you decide to do this, at the very entrance you will come up against an upturned truck. Behind the next truck, you will find a chaos so great, you will not be able to proceed further through it. About ten metres from the entrance, you will come across what used to be a floor hatch through which you can reach the engine room. Although the hatch-doors of what used to be the pilot station have long fallen off, I would not advise a visit to the engine room unless you are fully prepared and sure of yourself. There is very little space to move around in there and the only source of light is your torch. One deck higher you will

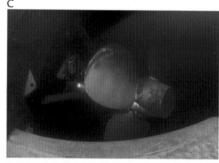

A - A divers shines his torch onto the back of an empty truck inside the hold of the Polish ferry Jan Heweliusz.

B - Upturned truck in the after hold of the sunken Polish ferry Jan Heweliusz.
One can still distinguish a small bouquet of flowers, through the window of the truck.
A mascot beloning ot

the truck driver or a hommage to the victims brought here by divers?

C - Divers in the bow Strahl rudder of the Jan Heweliusz.
Both the bow Strahl rudders were the last part of the vessel featured on television and press pictures, just before she totally capsized and sank.

find another breach in the stern, through which you can get into the wreck. The stern ramp is recognisable by the rail tracks that disappear into the wreck. Using this opening on the upper deck, you can visit practically the entire wreck to emerge through a small door under the bridge that is no longer there. The gigantic hull of the ferry, that is still easily recognisable as a ship, the huge rudder system at the stern and the enormous adjusting screws are highlights in themselves and ensure that your dive to the wreck will be quite unforgettable. If you don't venture into the wreck, this dive could even be labelled as 'suitable for beginners'. Over the years, a small number of fish have been attracted to the site. Cods can be seen around the site and in spring, lumpfish make the site even more inviting. The marine life attached to the body of the wreck is not very colourful, consisting exclusively of edible

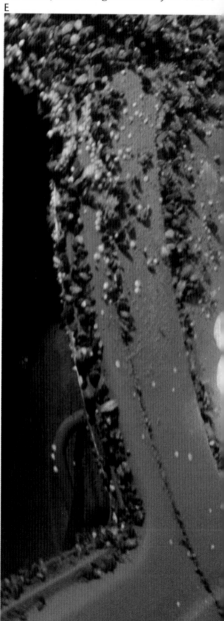

mussels. All diving expeditions that include a trip inside the wreck must be carefully planned and prepared. Besides standard diving equipment, special equipment is required. Apart from ample air reserves, each diver must be equipped with wreck-reels (guiding lines), additional lamps (of a type that can fully replace diving lamps), a reliable emergency lamp in 'jacket format', a helmet with emergency lamps attached, and a second, independent diving kit made up of the so-called 3-litre pony cylinder with its own regulator and finimeter, to serve as a last resort. The mere knowledge that if need be, one can produce air, "magically from up one's sleeve" goes a long way in helping divers keep a cool head in real or imagined crisis situations. All regulators used for such dives must have state-of-the art anti-freeze protection. Two independent regulators are absolutely necessary.

D - Davit of the sunken Polish ferry Jan Heweliusz. The under part of the entire davit was breached precisely at the welding seam.

E - The shell of this truck can be reached through a wide opening (10 X 20 metre large) on the right side of the boat. A clear cut was burnt through the ship's hull and ribs. The cut-out part of the hull was then carefully removed and laid away from the wreck.

F - Unlaunched lifeboat of the sunken Polish ferry Jan Heweliusz. There was no time to launch lifeboats as the vessel sank. Only the liferafts could be used.

G - Divers at the rounded entrance on the uppermost deck at the stern of the Jan Heweliusz. Maintenance work could be done through these shafts.

F

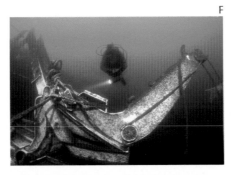

G

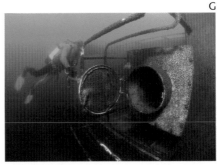

FEHMARN Text by Stefan Baehr

Island of Fehmarn

Puttgarden

FEHMARN

Katharinenhof

N

450 m

4 m

3 m

A

B

C

Fehmarn is Germany's Baltic island in the sun. After underwater visits to several small wrecks, one can find interesting shallow water diving sites here, close to the beach. The best place for such diving is the beach strip at Katharinenhof. This is a rather odd place, made up of a small group of farmhouses and a camping ground at the end of its single street.

Following the E47 highway, locally known as Vogelfluglinie 'line as-the-crow-flies', you reach the town on Fehmarn. This tiny town also serves as the island's capital. In the evening, one can go on an extended bout of pub

crawling. When coming up on the E47 highway, cross through the whole town and then follow the road signs for Katharinenhof. After about 4 km on a small meandering secondary road, you will have reached your destination. Just before the camping site, you will find the diving site and a diving centre that will fill your air cylinders and provide helpful information and diving tips.

The best thing to do is to get into the water, directly before the camping site. This is a typical beach dive, that is to say, you have to go quite a way from the shore before reaching the maximum possible diving depth of 8-9 metres. If you dive

towards the left, somewhat North of the slip-way system of the nearby camping site, you will find a huge block of rock. Local divers call it the 'Old Man'. It seems to lurk just under the surface, waiting for unsuspecting motor boats that ply the area using outboard motors. This dense mass of rock is only beloved by divers, especially underwater photographers who feel it is a fascinating subject. The entire seabed at this diving site is studded with rocky masses, that can sometimes reach a diameter of up to 7 metres. Between the rocks there are a number of pretty seaweed patches that sustain a wide variety of underwater life. In autumn, you will come across young cod, and sometimes a stately leaf fish. Herrings, needlefish, the northern sculpin, pipefish and all sorts of leaf fish, can be found all through the year, depending on their respective seasons.

This diving site is a closely kept secret by night diving fans and is a must for underwater macrophotographers. They

D

E

B - Rock blocks densely overgrown with algae are a major feature of the underwater landscape off Katherinenhof. The rock formations are interspersed by large expanses of sand.

C - The underwater landscape off Katharinenhof is densely overgrown with algae. The algae is interrupted here and there by sand patches and sea grass meadows that, unfortunately, are becoming a rarity in the Baltic Sea.

D - Sea weed meadows are interspersed by rocks overgrown with algae. The shallow depth of the water renders this diving site especially accessible to beginners.

E - The Four-whiskered rockling (Enchelypus cimbrius) is a member of the cod family and is the only kind of rockling to be found in the Baltic Sea. It generally inhabits areas featuring soft sandy seabeds.

F - The northern sculpin that lives on the seabed is a voracious predator. It generally waits motionless for its prey to be attracted by the pleasant coloured surroundings in which it lurks. It is a distant relative of the scorpionfish, although it does not have poisonous spines on its back.

A - Local Fehmarn divers have given this huge, impressive rock formation the nickname 'Old Man'. It lies just under the surface and has therefore been the bane of many an outboard motor. Below the surface, it provides an excellent subject for splendid photographs. The 'Old Man' is surrounded by sand and seaweed meadows.

flock here by night for the simple reason that it is during the night hours that the conditions are best for excellent photographs. One the way back to the point where the divers get into the water at the depth of 3-4 metres, you will come to a 400-metre long strip, strew with the remains of wrecks. Since these wreck remains are precisely at the indicated depth, they are difficult to miss. The wreck remains lie about 200 metres off the shore. The wreck remains include a few pieces of a port rail, a piece of a funnel and the remains of a bow The name of the wrecked vessel is unknown. This underwater site features completely easy diving. During the whole summer, you will do fine with just a 6 mm wet suit. All through from November to April, a dry suit should be used. Since the maximum depth of the dive is only 8 metres, a second breath regulator is not necessary at all. A 7 or 10-litre air cylinder should be more than sufficient. Bear in mind that all the equipment must also be carried over the beach, and therefore, the lighter, the better!

During night diving, you ought to have a lamp of a maximum of 35 Watts, since a stronger lamp would only spoil the wonderful atmosphere of the night dive. A small additional torch is however important, even if you may only need to avoid stumbling over the ever-present slippery rocks when you get out of the water.

In the summer months, especially, there is heavy marine traffic off the slipway system. For your own safety, you ought to signal your presence using a line

attached to a marking buoy on the surface.

You may have to negotiate a path over very slippery stones on the beach while going into and coming out of the water. The danger of slipping is multiplied near the slipway system.

This diving site is especially indicated for macrophotography. For best results, use a mirror reflex camera with a macro lens featuring a focal length of 50-60 mm. Wider focal ranges are not as effective and may even result in blurred pictures. For pictures like the ones in these pages, you must use an ultra-short focal range behind a semi-circular dome port. You will also need at least two flash bulbs to illuminate the whole underwater landscape. As you may have gathered, such photography is only for very serious photographers.

F

THE WRECK OF THE STENTRANS

Text by Stefan Baehr

DENMARK

Copenhagen

THE WRECK OF
THE STANTRANS

Kiel •

Fehmarn

GERMANY

• Rostock

N

0 m

7 m

21 m

7 m

21 m

Thursday, March 13, 1975 was the blackest day in the history of the Danish dredger *Sten Trans* owned by Transline. She was carrying sand ballast from Denmark to Kiel. Between the southern point of Langeland and the Fjords of Kiel, she encountered a severe storm. As the ballast cargo of the dredging ship was moving about in the hold under the influence of 7 to 9 force winds, a call for assistance at sea was sent out.

The sea rescue cruiser, *Theodor Heuss* put out in answer to the message, in a bid to rescue the men on board the *Sten Trans*. In the meanwhile, twelve of the fifteen men on board had abandoned the vessel and sought safety on a covered lifeboat. When the "Theodor Heuss" reached the location at 0515 hours, these 12 men were brought aboard. The captain and two steersmen who were still aboard the *Sten Trans* were brought aboard the rescue vessel by a Sea King helicopter sent from the *Theodor Heuss*.

At 0631 hours, the dredging ship capsized and sank.

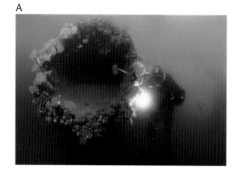

The *Sten Trans* lies in the western Baltic, between Langeland and Kiel in a very exposed location. Since there is no protection from the coast, stable good weather is an imperative prerequisite for any diving tour of the wreck. Strong currents are very frequent out here, and they sometimes change direction unexpectedly. Divers must then seek protection in the superstructure, although in general this poses no difficulty. A further problem is posed by the frequently very large waves at this site in the middle of the Baltic Sea. The ship lies on her port side at a depth of 21 metres. The topmost part of the wreck rises to about 7 metres beneath the surface of the sea.

The 'dredger' as she is often called, is 65-metres long, making her, to date, the largest wreck in the western Baltic. A wreck of the *Sten Trans* is well worth several dives. Given the fact that, from whichever direction the site is

approached, a very long boat trip is required, it is a good idea to plan the diving excursion as a full day outing, covering up to three dives.

The totally exposed location of the wreck also has its advantages, since it allows for a brisk exchange of water, ensuring that the wreck is rich in marine life. The entire wreck is overgrown with sea pink that sustain shore crabs and fish living on the seabed, such as the northern sculpin. In spring, one can also come across lumpfish. Now and then, a school of cod can be seen around the

A - View of the huge suction pipe of the Stentrans. Tons of silt from the seabed were pumped through this pipe and brought to the ship's hold. In this way, the vessel was used to keep access to ports in the shallow bottomed Baltic open.

B - The wreck of the Sten Trans, known as "The Suction dredger" in diving jargon, lies on its port side. Divers therefore approach the wreck from the starboard side, that now lies upwards.

Going into the pump room where the pipes were also stored, requires rather stronger nerves, and is undertaken with a certain amount of risk, although it may not be worth the trouble. Besides a greasy oil bubble that can make your diving suit stink for the rest of the day, and a couple of old pipes, you won't find anything exciting here. The same goes for the engine room.

It is, in any case, well worth your while to swim slowly alongside the entire superstructure and absorb a wide range of emotions as well as take photographs. Those interested in marine biology should also keep their eyes open in the superstructure, especially around the holds. At this wreck, one can frequently come across sea creatures that belong to a completely different underwater area, such as, for instance, the four-whiskered eel-pout.

From October to May a dry suit is

D - It is possible to dive between the wall of the bridge and the railing. Since the ship lies on its side, the railing appears on top in the picture. Below one can see the entrance to the bridge. It is easy to access the bridge.

E

C - The position of the bridge clearly shows that the ship lies on her side. The inside of the bridge is empty. Do not try to squeeze through the windows, the entrance is from above!

wreck.

The wreck is still in excellent condition. It is not broken apart and is relatively undamaged.

Visits to the inside of the ship can be undertaken by physically fit divers. Such divers can easily see the huge holds of the wreck without any problems. The floor of the holds are home to colonies of ascidians, making the holds well worth a visit. Close to the holds you can still see a few winches and a complete suction system.

A visit to the bridge also doesn't present any problems. Access to the bridge is from the starboard side or from the top of the vessel. Don't try to squeeze through the windows on the bridge since they are too narrow and you will damage the marine life growing around them. Furthermore by trying to squeeze through the windows you will ruin visibility by creating a turbulence of suspended particles.

highly recommended. A visit to this wreck also demands the use of underwater torches since it is very dark in the cargo holds of the sunken ship. The holds are however a good site to visit since they house a wide variety of marine life. A second, independent regulator is important and some diving centres make this an essential condition for all divers.

Macrophotography requires the use of a mirror reflex camera with a macro lens featuring a focal length of 50-60 mm. For an overall view of the wreck, the shortest available focal length must be used. Best results are obtained using a 14 mm or fish eye lens.

The ideal starting point for a visit to the wreck of the *Sten Trans* is the city of Kiel. The city has several diving centres that organise underwater tours of the wreck that has become a popular diving destination in northern Germany.

E - A huge winch lies in the area between the deck structures and the hold. It was once used for operating the suction system of the Sten Trans. The sea has recaptured the steelly technology of the ship and transformed it into a new biotope.

OESTERDAM Text by Harry Klerks

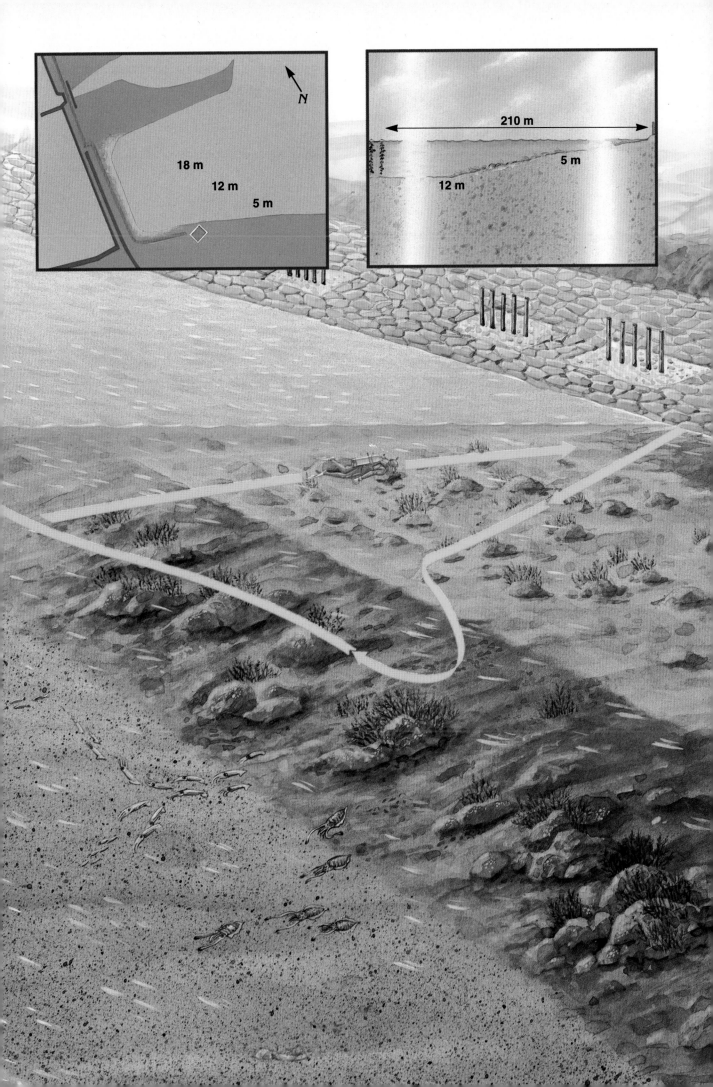

18 m

12 m

5 m

210 m

12 m

5 m

N

Oesterdam is a very peculiar diving spot, because of its location. It lies in a sheltered position, way inshore, and there is therefore hardly any current, although a channel runs through it almost up to the beach. This unique feature provides the depth required to attract larger marine animals. There are huge mussel banks south of the diving site, covering one fifth of the total surface area. These make for excellent feeding grounds for fish coming in from the North Sea, in search of suitable spawning locations. They keep following the winding tunnels until they can go no farther and then deposit their eggs. Commercial fishermen are well aware of this naturally, and divers must take special care to avoid the nets set just about everywhere.

The water here is the clearest in the entire Oostershelde and visibility of eight metres is not uncommon. Visibility is greatly reduced during the boom, that is to say, when an abundance of sunlight and warmth triggers an explosive proliferation of plancton that obscure the water. The bloom season generally starts in March and depends greatly on the number of sunlight hours.

Proceeding from Oesterdam towards Tholen, turn left immediately after passing the lock, then turn right and continue until you reach the dam. Then take the first road to the left and park close to the dam. Change into diving gear and climb over the dike. From the dike you will see small breaches between rock formations, affording access to deeper waters. Once in the water, descend slowly to admire the rock formations overgrown with Japanese Sargasso weed and the little crabs and seaweed shrimp, glass prawn and spider

A

B

C

A - Hermit-crabs (Pagurus bernhardus) *can be found everywhere in both deep and shallow waters in the Oosterschelde.*

B - Boat harbour on the sea front, close to the oyster bank, near the diving site.

C - *The common cuttlefish (Sepia officinalis) comes to the Oosterschelde in spring to spawn.*

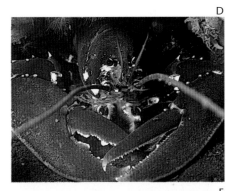
D

E

across a sea anemone or a northern blood starfish. You will almost always encounter jellyfish, moon jellyfish, rhizostonme and compass jellyfish as well as the little sea gooseberry, a common feature in these waters, that will give you a show of beautiful coloured patterns if you direct your torch to it. A little later, you will come across a metal bar imbedded in the bottom. Last year, it was covered with long finned squid eggs that look like opaque sausages. A friend of mine reported that most of them have hatched and that he was surrounded by at least a hundred of them during a recent night dive. At this point, you should turn back and move into shallower waters at a depth of between 6 and 3 metres. You will notice a little reef that provides a home to lobster and tadpole fish. Just beyond the reef, there is a field of seaweed, above which swim greater pipefish and schools of black gobies. When swimming above the sand, you might come across primita. In the spring, lumpsuckers will lay and guard their eggs here, because of the weak current that has also made this area an ideal ground for diving tests.

The water can get quite muddy and you are well advised to avoid this site on weekends.

D - *An encounter with a lobster (Homarus gammarus) is sought after by all divers.*

E - *The Chameleon prawn (Hippolyte varians). This prawn changes colour to blend into its surroundings.*

F - *Aesop prawn (Pandalus montagui). A keen eye is required to spot this prawn.*

G - *Plumose anemones (Metridium senile) grow on sandy bottoms and open entirely in the nutrient-rich in-coming current.*

crabs scurrying amongst the rocks are you approach. At 3 metres, you will notice a small drop off to 12 metres. This is the beginning of the nicest part of the dive. Do not attempt to go below 12 metres, as the lack of current ensures that any body movement will turn the water into a muddy mess with zero visibility. Remain above 12 metres and swim towards the right. At this point, you are in the greenhouse of the Oosterschelde and you will encounter a wide variety of fish from the common cuttlefish to the long finned squid. You will also find banks of dead oysters and shells that are used as a base by various fauna, such as star tunicates, tube sea squirts and small snakelock anemones.

Further right you will notice that the water gets deeper still and the build up is replaced by oyster banks. Lobsters burrow in tunnels beneath these banks and quite like private security guards, they will defend their property with their claws. The brill, on the sandy bed, is totally covered, watching for passing unsuspecting prey. At the 18 metre mark you will notice cultured banks of hanging mussels. These ropes are entirely covered with mussels and are attached to a web of rafters. Bass are very active here and chase after schools of poor cod. Negotiating a path back through the strands of cultured mussels, go back to the drop off and swim along it. You will notice that it becomes smoother and shallower. At this point, you are on a sandbank and there is very little of interest. On occasion, you may come

F

G

ZEELANDRUNG Text by Harry Klerks

10 m

20 m

25 m

Pillar1

Pillar 2

N

10 m

20 m

25 m

0 m

10 m

20 m

25 m

Most diving sites in Benelux are located in Zeeland, (Sea Land) and therefore it will come as no surprise that it is in this area that most divers congregate. A major part of Zeeland consists of a delta with lots of diving hot spots, and on a sunny June weekend, you may encounter about 5000 fellow divers.

The best spots for diving are concentrated around the Oosterschelde. At some spots you will find a 10 km stretch of sandbanks, formed and reshaped by tidal currents that provide the sandbanks with a fresh supply of plankton every six hours.

This constant supply of plankton renders the Oosterschelde a good feeding ground for mussels and oysters, that in turn provide food for crabs and starfish that are eaten by other predators. All this supports a rich ecosystem in these cold waters. Sometimes, you can even

encounter a seal enjoying an afternoon nap on the beach. The diving sites around the Oosterschelde are easily accessible by road. Diving usually starts from the shore. Most diving site are exposed to currents and it is advisable to start diving half an hour before the tide turns and get out of the water about fifteen minutes after the tide has changed. It is strictly forbidden to disturb underwater plants or animals and bring them to the surface. Only licensed divers

are allowed to dive in these waters and a diving license may be obtained against a fee of 47 Dutch Florins at any post office. Stab jackets are compulsory and it is a good idea to carry a good torch when diving.

After parking your car and changing into diving gear, take the stairs down, to the right of the dike. You need to cross the dike to reach the water on the other side. It is advisable to get into the water beneath the bridge. At high tide, this is

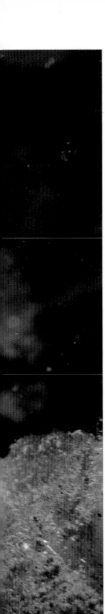

very easy, but divers must be very careful at low tide since seaweed growing on the ground can make the entrance very slippery indeed. There are very few divers to be found outside the water at this time!, especially during weekends. Once in the water, divers set course for the first pillar of the bridge and then go below the surface. Underwater, divers are greeted by sargasso weed, stretching in a thick forest from the underwater rocks up to the surface. Rocks lying at depth of over two metres are overgrown with various kinds of sea anemones to a depth of about a further two metres. Lower yet, there is a blanket of sand sprinkled with various shellfish and brittle starfish. At this point, divers are at a depth of about four metres and still heading towards the first pillar of the bridge. Along the way, you will notice small rock formations covered with little anemones. It is not uncommon to come across spidercrabs on the seaweed, trying to catch plankton with their long arms. At this point, you should descend to the foundation of the pillar. It has been eroded by the current and is home to various underwater creatures. Lobsters hide in crevices and now and again you may come across a large conger that has made its home in one of the deeper caves. Sometimes, lobster and shrimp live in symbiosis. At the very bottom of the pillar, divers will find a carpet of mussels, brittle starfish, blood starfish and now and again, a sea urchin.
The pillar itself is entirely covered with

C - Juvenile lump sucker (Cyclopterus lumpus). A rather rare encounter.

D - The oyster bank have become an oasis of life.

E - Common cuttlefish (Sepia officinalis). A couple has met, and mating can begin.

F - Snakelock anemones (Sagartiogeton undatus) are everywhere and are a pleasure to the eye.

yellow sea squirt, teeming with marine creatures, including green crabs, anemones spider crabs, various kinds of shrimp and nudibranches, such as green elisia, antiopelle, white coypella and grey sea slugs.
The pillar is crowned by a platform. Divers are at the bottom of it, naturally, and the colours switch from white to orange and red. The overgrowth mostly features various kinds of anemones. Grey mullet and sea bass are common here. At this point, divers generally turn around and follow the same route back to end the first dive. The second dive will be similar to the first, around the second pillar of the Zeeland bridge. This dive is recommended for divers with 2 star higher diving skills as the current can be strong. We spotted sea horses on several occasions to the right of the pillar, at a depth of about 12 metres. If you are a non-vegetarian, we really recommend that you stop at one of the local restaurants to indulge in a serving of mussels and French fries, that will give you a real taste of the true flavour of Zeeland!

A - The short-spined sea-scorpion (Myoxocelophalus scorpius) has a flat head. Its spines are slightly venomous.

B - Red eye crab or velvet crab (Necora puber). The male will clutch the female until the female has cast off her skin, since mating cannot take place before.

WEMELDINGE   Text by Harry Klerks

3 m

29 m

35 m

3 m

29 m

35 m

300 m

600 m

This is another diving spot located at the Oosterschelde. The boobies have an excellent reputation because of the beautiful fauna and flora. It is an ideal diving spot for the macro photographer, who preferably should use lens 1to1 up to 1to3. The visibility in the spot is variable depending on the season. The reason for this is mainly the direction and strength of the prevailing winds. During low tide, large areas are dry, sometimes up to 100 meters wide. This dry area consists of a very fertile mud. Winds from the north during low tide will stir up this muck and cloud the water, which decreases the visibility considerably.

The Boobs are easily found on the dike, proceeding towards the Zeeland Bridge. They are the two dikes going

A

out into the sea. The lock between the Boobs serve to pump water out of the polder. You should park to the left of the dike and get into the water from the little beach, just alongside the dike. It is a good idea to carry a heavy-duty flashlight and a little extra air, bearing in mind that you will have to swim about 50 metres in shallow water, after which it will gradually get deeper. The drop off starts at about 3 metres.

B

You may come across several sea bass that are not at all shy, probably because they are often fed by the divers who frequent these waters.

Descending deeper still, you will find small white and orange fields of plumose anemones. At this point, the water gets decidedly deeper and at 15 metres, you will notice large blocks of peat, that are literally teeming with marine life: the entire surface of these blocks are covered with little anemones, every little nook and cranny is home to some kind of underwater animal. Black gobies abound, but lobsters too have managed to carve themselves a place.

The marine life around the peat blocks include hairy sea squirt, dirty sea squirt, spira bryzoan, tube sponges, mixilla, common brittle stars, andresia

C

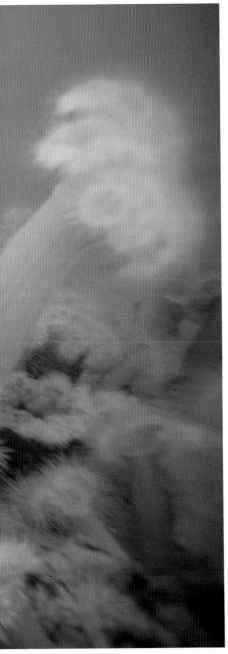

amongst which crabs and shrimp hide, although they still seem to fall prey to butterfish.

In spring, shoals of cuttlefish congregate here to mate and spawn. At a depth of 32 metres, you will reach a sandy platform. You will still come across little peat formations, carpeted with orange striped anemones and dotted with flower heads and organ pipes, over which little bob-tailed cuttlefish swim. As you approach the 35-metre mark, you will also encounter plaice, and if you're lucky, even sole. Keep to your right and continue swimming for about three minutes, until you reach a large block, entirely covered with orange encrusting anemones. At the rear of this block there is a cave-like opening that is home to huge lobster that must weigh at least 8 lbs. The lobster may seem quite peaceful and oblivious to what is around it but divers are advised to keep a safe distance and to refrain from touching it – a crushed finger at a depth of 35 m is not a happy prospect!

At this point, you should turn back and start heading towards the shore, while ascending for about 6 metres to the 29-metre mark. Aiming your torch towards the sandy seabed in a southwesterly direction, you should see the remains of an old fyke. It is generally covered with eggs of the common cuttlefish. Depending on the how much the eggs have developed, you can shine your torch through these eggs and see the small little squidlike fish moving very fast in all directions inside the egg. Under no circumstances

should these eggs be disturbed in any way. The male common cuttlefish is about 40 cm long and doubles in length when its two long tentacles are extended. When disturbed or threatened, they will shoot away, leaving a black cloud of squid ink behind them. This is a sign that you have outstayed your welcome and should take your leave. Care must be taken while ascending.

Fykes, attached to a net of about 8 metres have been set a little past the large peat blocks.

While following the same route back, pay close attention to the tide, since currents can be quite strong here. At high tide, fishermen use the quay to cast for fish and it is therefore advisable to move a little more to the right before resurfacing.

E

F

D

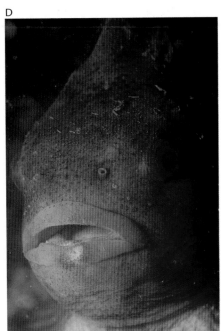

A - Underwater scene featuring a lobster hole.

B - A shrimp typical of the Oosterschelde.

C - A hermit-crab covered with barnacles on a starfish (Asteria rubens).

D - Female lumpsuckers (Cyclopterus lumpus) swims into the Oosterschelde to spawn. The male protects the eggs from predators. As soon as the young fish have hatched, it will return to the open sea.

E - Mud-sagartia (Sagartia troglodytes) with hermit-crab (Pagurus bernhardus).

F - Sea pink or plumose anemones (Metridium senile) are found in various colours at this diving site.

UNITED KINGDOM AND IRELAND

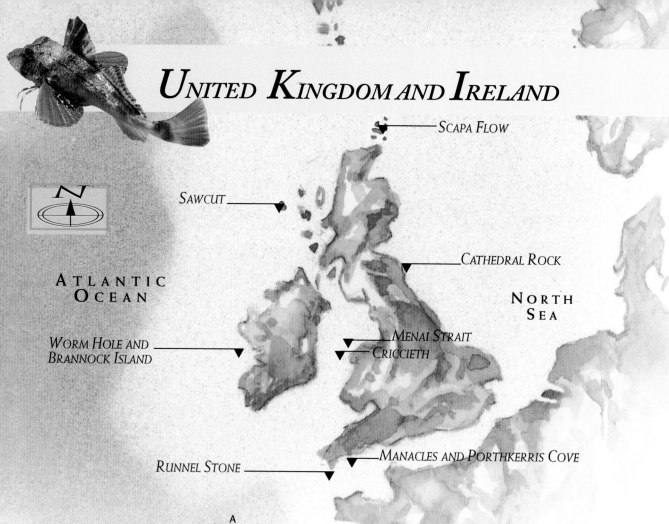

SCAPA FLOW

N

SAWCUT

CATHEDRAL ROCK

ATLANTIC
OCEAN

NORTH
SEA

WORM HOLE AND
BRANNOCK ISLAND

MENAI STRAIT
CRICCIETH

RUNNEL STONE

MANACLES AND PORTHKERRIS COVE

A

Being islands, United Kingdom and Ireland offer the choice of two seas and one ocean to dive in and have an incredible range of coastal topography to choose from. The infrastructure for visiting divers is excellent and most coastal towns feature diving centres, charter boats, training and equipment hire. Diving is available around the length of both island coasts, but for this guide we have sought out the very best areas and the finest dive

sites around them.
The selection and location of these areas is very much dictated by the routing of the Gulf Stream that bathes the south western peninsula of England, the south of Ireland and continues up the western coast of the UK through the Irish Sea to the offshore islands of the Hebrides before curling around the north of Scotland towards Norway. As the Gulf Stream divides around the south western peninsula the warmer, clearer waters it carries propagates a diversity of indigenous and visiting marine life not generally found elsewhere around the coastline. The headlands and offshore reefs are bombarded by nutrients borne by the strong tides on both coasts, feeding a multitude of species of anemones, soft and stony corals and invertebrate life. These organisms appear to paint the rocks with carpets of colour and can give an almost tropical feel to many dives as you swim among gorgonian fan corals, Ross coral, cup corals and walls of brilliantly hued plumose and jewel anemones. Fish life is profuse with shoals of bass and mackerel, reef dwelling wrasse, flatfish, blennies, scorpionfish, tope, sharks and a variety

of foreign visitors from warmer southern waters. The roasting summer of 1995 brought with it triggerfish, sunfish, leather-back turtles and in 1998 more than 500 basking sharks were recorded off the coast of Cornwall during the month of May! The variety is almost endless and will keep a photographer or marine life enthusiast busy for months!
The South Western Approaches represent the gateway to merchant shipping entering the English Channel or continuing up the west coast to the major trading ports of Bristol, Cardiff or Liverpool. This area has been one of the world's busiest shipping lanes for hundreds of years and the coasts of Cornwall and southern Ireland have been the first landfall and the site of

B

C

D

an amazing variety of invertebrates – a real sponge city!

Wales also offers exhilarating offshore diving with a choice of high energy wall diving and a number of wrecks. Finally we go to Scotland where we discover the best beach diving to be found on the eastern North Sea coast, explore the battle ships of Scapa Flow and travel to the westernmost dive site in the UK at St. Kilda for some of the most challenging Atlantic diving available. While these waters offer so much to the visiting diver, they should be treated with respect even on high summer days when the water resembles a sheet of glass. Sadly, there are a number of diver fatalities every year, many of which could have been avoided with a little forward planning and local knowledge. The tides can be vicious in many areas and the weather can change quickly, especially on the Atlantic coasts.

To keep your visit memorable for the right reasons, dives should not be planned without complete details of tides and weather forecasts as well as the benefit of local advice that is freely available from the Coast Guard and the many diving centres. Alternatively, you can choose to dive with one of the many day boats or live-aboard boats that operate within these areas and leave the planning to a skipper who deals with these waters on a daily basis. Whatever your choice, you will be surprised at the variety and dramatic contrasts these areas have to offer.

tragedy for many mariners. Armada ships, East Indiamen, liners, merchant and convoy shipping from both World Wars have met their fate along these coastlines. There are literally hundreds of recorded losses with many still awaiting discovery either by chance or through dedicated research. In Scotland there is a wreck graveyard of a different kind in Scapa Flow. It was here that the German Imperial fleet of the Great War was scuttled following the Armistice and is one of a handful of locations world-wide where divers can swim amongst these monstrous battleships.

The diversity of diving sites is remarkable and will offer something for all divers, regardless of their experience or particular interest in the underwater world. The choice ranges from sheltered bays and estuaries for relaxed diving and exploration to the high energy offshore sites on the Atlantic and Channel coasts, reserved for more experienced divers in

search of challenging waters.
In the south west of England we will visit the infamous Runnel stone, a spectacular reef on the edge of the Atlantic that has been responsible for the loss of 27 ships, the Manacles, another tide-swept reef rich in marine life, that is also the graveyard of several wrecks and finally the more relaxed pleasures of a beach dive from the famous Lizard Peninsula.

The Irish coast is bathed by the sometimes unforgiving swells of the Atlantic, but in the right conditions, provides some of the best diving in Europe. We describe the sensational Arran islands and the Skelligs islands - real Wild West diving. In Wales, we search for something completely different in the Menai Straits where the combination of strong currents and nutrient rich water creates a high bio-diversity habitat that, while not perhaps providing sparkling visibility, supports

E

A - Along the rugged and granitic coastline of England's Southwest peninsula some superb dive sites can be found.

B - The block ships sunk at Scapa Flow were used to block narrow passages of water to incoming enemy ships.

C - Anglerfish (Lophius piscatorius) prefer the base of cliffs, next to a gravel seabed where they lie waiting for prey.

D - Plumose anemones (Metridium senile) compete with jewel anemones (Corynactis viridis) and soft corals (Alcyonium digitatum) for space to feed and reproduce in the nutrient rich waters.

E - The well camouflaged top knot flatfish (Zeugopterus punctatus) is common on all reefs.

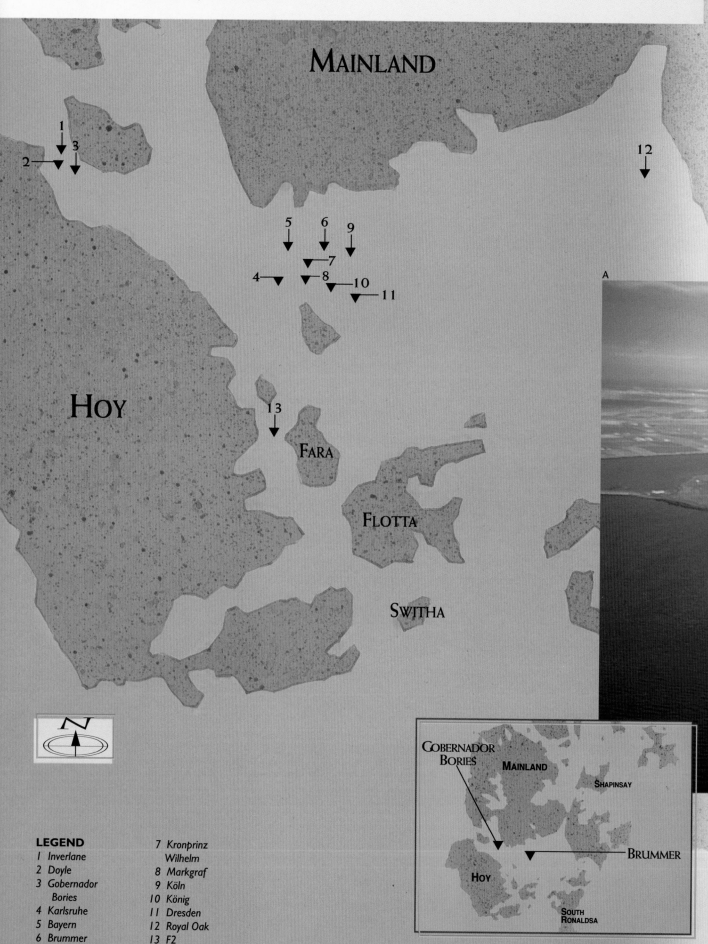

SCAPA FLOW Text by Lawson Wood

MAINLAND

HOY

FARA

FLOTTA

SWITHA

LEGEND

1 Inverlane	7 Kronprinz Wilhelm
2 Doyle	8 Markgraf
3 Gobernador Bories	9 Köln
4 Karlsruhe	10 König
5 Bayern	11 Dresden
6 Brummer	12 Royal Oak
	13 F2

GOBERNADOR BORIES

MAINLAND

SHAPINSAY

HOY

BRUMMER

SOUTH RONALDSA

Sitting in the early morning calm, while the cold air of daybreak was leaving a slight foggy residue around the dive boat, we could see no land, or in fact any other living thing, except a tiny orange marker buoy with afrayed bit of line attached. Not exactly an auspicious start to diving in what is considered to be the best wreck diving area in Europe, but Scapa Flow ranks as one of the top five wreck diving locations in the world.

The natural harbour of Scapa Flow in the Orkney Islands has the largest concentration of shipwrecks in the northern hemisphere.

We were about to dive one of those ancient eerie and spectacular war horses, dropping through 30 metres of

B

C

excitement as you approach the Orkney Islands by ferry. The initial huge land mass that looms up out of the early morning mist is the Island of Hoy and as they approach the first of several entrances to Scapa Flow, visitors can see the early signs of the derelict rusting hulks.

These hulks were ships which were deliberately sunk to block up unauthorised entry by the enemy into Scapa Flow and are known as 'Blockships'.

As well as these blockships, the remains of the interred German High Seas Battle Fleet lie deep beneath the surface, alongside one of the most famous wrecks in British naval history, HMS Royal Oak.

water (100 ft) to arrive near the bows of a former German light cruiser scuttled in 1919 in a bay set amidst some of the most dramatic scenery in Europe.

Considered by many to be impregnable to attack, the bay of Scapa Flow covering some 190 sq. km (120 square miles) is completely sheltered by a ring of protective islands.

Situated 25 km (15 miles) north of the Scottish mainland, it can be accessed using the daily car ferry from Scrabster or by regular flight to Kirkwall airport from Edinburgh and Aberdeen.

There is always a sense of mounting

A - The Churchill Barriers link the Orkney mainland to Lamb Holm, Glims Holm, Burray and South Ronaldsay. they were built by Italian prisoners of war to replace the ineffective block ships.

B - The schooner Reginald was one of the casualties of the war: she was sunk deliberately as a block ship in 1915.

C - The naval cemetery at Lyness holds the graves of many different nationalities.

A

A - The Hindenberg was one of the most famous of all German Battleships, seen here at rest on the seabed. The Hindenberg was eventually raised and salvaged. However three other great battleships still lie below these northern waters.

B - After several months of being blocked within the confines of Scapa Flow, at orders from Admiral Von Reuter, the captured German High Seas Fleet was deliberately scuttled in Scapa Flow on 21st June 1919.

C - The light destroyers quickly sank to the bottom of Scapa Flow, many in waters too deep to be safely raised, although a large number of the vessels in shallow waters were salvaged in later years.

D - Sheltered against strong currents, the former interior of the block ship Inverlane was lit by the many holes in the top deck. Only half of the ship lies in the Burra Sound, the rear half was salvaged and used in the construction of another ship in England.

E - Once completely open and safe for divers, the Inverlane was a classic wreck, that could be visited at any tide, just waiting to be explored.

One of the most evident of the blockships is the 8,900-ton Inverlane that spans Burra Sound. Although it once looked like a classic shipwreck from the symbols on admiralty charts, with her prow and forward masts clear of the water and the aft lost to view, the promise of dives to come, the Inverlane has now collapsed in on itself and is considered too dangerous for safe penetration. However, the three blockships adjacent to the Inverlane are all superb dives. The *Tabarka, Doyle* and *Gobernador Bories* are all considered to be the most photogenic of all the wrecks, with the *Gobernador Boreis* being the most popular. The *Gobernador Boreis* is just one of a series of 43 'block ships' weighing over 100,000 gross tons which were sunk deliberately during WWI and WWII to block the navigable entrances to Scapa Flow against enemy shipping, mainly German submarines. Scapa Flow was also further guarded by shore batteries, submarine nets and constant

C

naval patrols. After the daring attack on *HMS Royal Oak* by the U47 in 1939, Scapa Bay was further protected on the eastern shores by a series of causeways which were built by Italian prisoners of war. These causeways now link all of the eastern islands and are known collectively as the Churchill Barriers. On Lamb's Holm a former WWII building has been wonderfully painted to recreate the interior of an Italian Chapel. The Italian Chapel is now fully restored and well worth a visit. A brief look at Scapa Flow's history will explain why the ships are here and what makes them so interesting. At the end of the First World War, the German High Seas Fleet was brought to Scapa Flow to be interred. Admiral Ludwig von Reuter took advantage of the internment to save the Imperial Fleet from further disgrace and being convinced that war conditions were to be reinstated decided to scuttle the fleet after the Armistice on 21st June 1919. Whilst the British fleet left that morning on exercise after seven months of confinement, von Reuter decided to save their countrymens' honour and

D

B

deliberately scuttled the fleet.
At 11a.m. the skeleton crews on board opened condensers, valves and pipes. Within four hours, most of the ships had sunk from view, others were beached and many flipped upside down on their way to the sea bed. 25 of these ships were salvaged by Cox & Danks during a 20 month period starting in 1924. At present there are 3 German battleships, 4 light cruisers, a WW2 destroyer (F2), 2 submarines, 27 large sections of remains and salvage equipment, 16 known British wrecks, 32 block ships and 2 British Battleships (the *Vanguard* and the *Royal Oak*), as well as a further 54 sections of wreckage, as yet unidentified.

Now more than eighty years after the sinking, the wrecks are still making history, as one of the greatest dive attractions in Europe.

Conditions vary tremendously during the season and at the centre of the Scapa Flow, visibility is low and natural light scarce. Torches should be used at all times and work-up dives must be undertaken before attempting the deeper battleships. This is one of the reasons many photographers prefer the block ships at the entrance to Burra Sound, where the average depth is half that of the German warships. There is subsequently much more light, more interesting marine growth and much clearer water as the tidal race at Burra Sound sweeps all sedimentation particles away. But this also means that you have only limited time on these wrecks and then only at slack tide. The Burra Sound wrecks are the most photogenic and although there is not so much mystique attached them, as the scuttled German fleet, the blockships

A - The kelp and algae encrusted steel decking ribs make a perfect backdrop for the easy exploration of the block ship Gobernador Bories. This section of the hull also protects divers from the strong currents which sweep the wreck.

17 m

0 m

17 m

A

B

C

B - The bows of this blockship are covered in kelp as it lies in only 15 metres of water. The water quality around these blockships is the clearest in Scapa Flow.

C - The steel ribs are all that remains of the wooden wheelhouse on the Gobernador Bories. Due to the almost constant tidal currents, the spars are completely covered in marine life and of great interest to divers.

are considered to be the best for photography.

The most popular is the *Gobernador Bories*, formerly known as the *Wordsworth*, weighing in at 2332 tons. She was an iron single-screw steamer built in 1882 at West Hartlepool and registered in Punta Arenas in Chile. The *Gobernador Bories* was sunk in 1915

and is considered to be the most popular of the blockships with divers, since her sinking dates from around the same period as the internment of the German Fleet. Now lying in 16 metres of water, the hull is fairly well broken up and angled over to port. The main wooden decking is all gone now, leaving the metal spars all covered in kelp, soft corals and hydroids. The bow and stern are almost completely intact and the propeller is still visible. The underside of the bow is completely covered by plumose anemones (*Metridium senile*). Due to the open aspect of the wreck, there is quite a lot of shelter from the current and divers can enter the main part of the forward section through two fairly open areas in the tangled wreckage. The inside of the hull is quite open and uncluttered except for the families of ballan wrasse which follow you into the ship. The upright spars near the stern feature pincushion starfish, hydroids, small seasquirts and red and brown algae. This dive should only be undertaken at slack water and then only on advice from the dive boat skipper.

A - A diver approaches the rear decking of the Brummer. Lying on her starboard side the rear section is fairly intact and covered in marine growth.

B - The bows of the German light cruiser Dresden lie on her side and perfectly frame this visiting diver. The hull of the ship is now covered with soft coral and plumose anemones.

C - These are the twin 20mm anti-aircraft guns which were salvaged from the torpedo recovery vessel F2 which sank on her mooring in 1946. The salvage vessel YC21 also sank at her mooring and now divers can enjoy both wrecks at the same time.

18 m

36 m

33 m

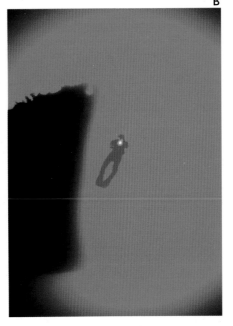

Smaller amounts of wreckage are found on the sites of the former *Rotherfield*, *Urmstone Grange*, *Ronda* and *Budrie*. The blockships located to the east, lying alongside the Churchill Barriers are used for training dives and for easy exploration and photography. These ships are all topped with kelp, their open decking spars now covered in small anemones, sea urchins and starfish and surrounded by resident groups of ballan wrasse.

In deeper and calmer waters in central Scapa Bay, the *Brummer* is just one of the four remaining German light cruisers and three battleships which were scuttled under the orders of Admiral Ludwig von Reuter in 1919. Through the descending gloom, the graceful arch of the sharp bows approach us and we drop to the stony seabed to gaze upwards in awe at this massive ship lying on her starboard side.

The hull is completely festooned in plumose anemones (Metridium senile) and feather starfish (*Antedon bifida*). From here we swam along the now vertical decking, past the forward 5.9 inch gun and approached the superstructure which is mostly collapsed. The central section of the ship is now completely destroyed, blasted apart by salvage divers, however the stern is mainly intact and the other 5.9 inch gun can be found. Maximum depth is 36 metres (120 ft)

and all too soon it is time to make our way up the mooring buoy line. The other destroyers nearby and in near identical condition are the *Koln*, *Dresden* and the *Karlsruhe*. The *Koln* has a very distinctive gun amid sections and is considered the most intact, the *Karlsruhe* is the shallowest at only 26 metres (86 ft) to the seabed. Although the *Karlsruhe* is fairly well broken up, the wreck is generally used as the first dive to allow divers to build up to the deeper wrecks and to get a first taste of the conditions and hazards that await those who dive Scapa Flow. All of these light cruisers lie on their side and are still very recognisable.

The larger battleships *Konig*, *Kronprinz Wilhelm* and *Markgraf* are in much deeper water and all are lying upside down, making examination and photography difficult.

In between dives, the dive boats often anchor on the jetty at Lyness, the former Naval Base on the Island of Hoy. Incidentally, the wreck of the F2, a German Torpedo boat and her salvage barge, that sank in 1968, also lie nearby. The salvage company had just removed a set of guns from the F2 and had tied tight onto the stricken vessel (at low tide). The crew went off to celebrate their good fortune at being able to raise the guns and left their booty to the fate of a six metre (20 ft) rising tide, that sunk their barge (and their booty), making for two very nice diveable wrecks (and both with guns). The wrecks are attached by rope and are close enough and small enough to visit in a single dive.

A - The ancient "Carley Liferafts" could not be used to rescue the crew of the Royal Oak, since a large number of them had been damaged in an earlier storm and were lying useless, strapped to the deck.

B - This cable reel from the deck is now partly buried in the silt under the hull of the Royal Oak.

C - HMS Royal Oak is seen here with her sister ships in 1939.

D - On the 14th October 1939, the Royal Oak was torpedoed and sunk in under 10 minutes.

E,G The pieces of ordance that once constituted the firepower of the Royal Oak, now rest silent and completely encrusted in marine growth.

The Lyness Museum in the old pump house for the naval base has an excellent pictorial history of the island's war efforts and a new multi-media display is open to the public in an old oil storage tank. 20 years after the German Fleet was scuttled, on the night of October 14th, 1939, the 188 metre (600 ft) battleship *Royal Oak* was at anchor in the sheltered bay of Scapa Flow in the Orkney Islands. Her duties were to protect Kirkwall and the British fleet from aerial attack. Scapa Flow was considered impenetrable because of the narrow passages between the reefs and islands. Likely attack would be expected only from the skies. However, nobody told this to the commander of the U47, Günther Prien, who stealthily approached Scapa Flow in what is considered by many to be one of the bravest feats in naval history and at the dead of night, sunk the *Royal Oak*. Just six weeks after the start of hostilities during the war, the *Royal Oak* sank in only ten minutes, taking over 800 men with her.
Fully armed and now lying almost

C

D

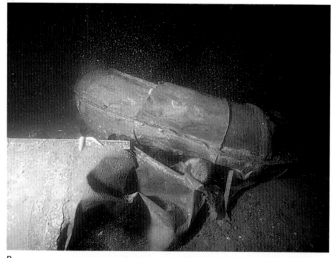

A

B

E

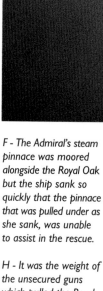

F

upside down, supported by her massive 15 inch guns, the *Royal Oak* is a poignant reminder to the futility of war. Surrounded by the unused Carley life rafts, the admiral's pinnace was dragged under with her and lies alongside the hulk of the ship which still leaks fuel oil to the surface even after all these years.
The bridge and conning tower are largely destroyed. Many port holes are still closed and the anti-aircraft guns are now encrusted with marine life.
The *Royal Oak* is now a designated war grave and is protected under Naval Law. Diving on her is strictly forbidden and consequently, she is THE ship most divers want to visit.
Scapa Flow is considered by many to be the best wreck diving location in the northern hemisphere, yet the

F - The Admiral's steam pinnace was moored alongside the Royal Oak but the ship sank so quickly that the pinnace that was pulled under as she sank, was unable to assist in the rescue.

H - It was the weight of the unsecured guns which pulled the Royal Oak over to her starboard side. The barrels ramming upright into the seabed, now support much of the superstructure.

G

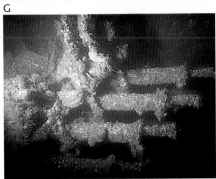

H

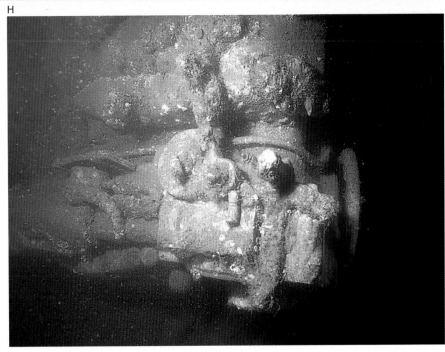

conditions encountered while diving to visit these ancient leviathans are extreme and hazardous. Diving at the edge of the safe scuba diving limits in low visibility and cold northern waters means that extra care should be taken at all times. If you follow the rules, you will be amply rewarded with the fabulous sight of this fascinating slice of European history.

SAWCUT Text by Lawson Wood

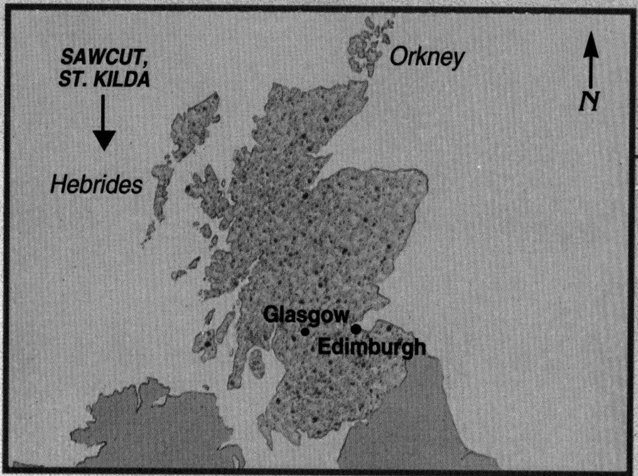

0 m

10 m

28 m

Soay

St. Kilda

SAWCUT

Dun

N

10 m

28 m

60 m

A

B

Eighty kilometres due west of Tarbert on the Isle of Harris in the Outer Hebrides and over 160 km from mainland Scotland the St. Kilda Archipelago is the westernmost inhabited island in Europe, although its population is mainly limited to military personnel and seasonal wardens for the National Trust for Scotland. The main group of islands are Hirta, Dun, Soay and Boreray. Most of the references to the islands known as St. Kilda refer to Hirta, the largest of the islands. St. Kilda or Skilder (from the Norse word for 'Shield') have provided a safe haven for many ships blown off course along the western Hebrides of Scotland - even the Spanish Armada lost ships around these islands. In 1930, the native population was finally evacuated from these extremely remote islands due to deprivation and disease. Once viewed as

C

an oddity by Victorian Society, the native population sadly fell victim to a spate of diseases brought to the island by visiting mainlanders. Over many generations of living on these islands, the locals developed extremely strong ankle bones and almost prehensile toes, since they climbed the cliffs bare feet to catch their staple food of sea birds and eggs. The Islands are so effectively cut off from all civilisation that there are even indigenous species of animals which are found nowhere else in Europe such as the St. Kilda Wren, St. Kilda Mouse and Soay Sheep. The National Trust for Scotland is busy renovating many of the former village houses during the calmer summer months on the main island of Hirta. The archipelago is only accessible by boat and the arduous journey to these lonely islands seemingly in the middle of the Atlantic Ocean, may take over 36 hours in rough seas. First glimpses of the islands are awesome, as they loom out of the sea mist and it is always with relief that the live-aboard dive boats pull into sheltered Village Bay. Sadly, because of the mainly inclement weather encountered so far offshore, much of the diving will occur within the confines of Village Bay and the area around the island of Dun. The Island of Dun is a national bird sanctuary and no one is allowed to set foot on the island, however it is the underwater terrain which attracts divers and in particular the Sawcut. The Sawcut is a vertical slice into the inshore side of Dun which bottoms out at 28 metres amidst a tumble of massive boulders at the entrance and gradually gets shallower as you progress the 60 metres or so into

the headland until the water is around 10 metres deep. The average width of the canyon is only 3 metres making it quite spectacular as the underwater visibility is always twice that of the outside wall. The kelp forest in these off-shore islands reaches depths of 25 metres and fringe the sides and upper reaches of the canyon. With the reduction of light, the kelp forest stops at the edge of the overhanging lip of the canyon and from here on down the walls are covered in soft corals (Alcyonium digitatum), jewel anemones (Corynactis viridis), sea squirts and numerous species of starfish. Everywhere you look the walls light up with colour and although a torch is always recommended on the dive, it is rarely needed due to the clarity and the

D

amount of light which streams through the surface waters. Small schools of fish hover around the entrance to the Sawcut, octopus are usually encountered amidst the boulder strewn seabed and seals are always an additional bonus on this dive as they often venture in to see what the divers are up to. The underwater landscape beneath the mooring in Village Bay is also interesting at night, with many octopus, shrimp and hermit crabs. Village Bay is completely sheltered from the worst of the Atlantic storms and offers safe anchorage for your live-aboard dive boat. Dive charter boat is the only way out to the Islands as the aerial trips made by Bristows helicopters are reserved for emergency use, mail and British Army personnel. The main island of Hirta is well worth

exploring on foot and you should make the effort to climb to the top, the views are quite spectacular. The vertical cliffs here are the highest in the British Isles and the noise from the nesting seabirds in the spring is almost deafening. It is true to say that the hardest to reach diving locations also yield the highest potential for dives of above average quality.

E

A - The island of Hirta (known commonly as St. Kilda) is seen here, photographed from the island of Dun. The natural harbour of the bay offers perfect anchorage and is a good base from which to explore these fascinating islands.

B - Here a diver explores one of the many submarine cliffs covered in soft corals, sponges and anemones.

C - A juvenile saithe (Pallachius virens), hides within the protective reach of the stinging tentacles.

D - Lesser spotted dogfish (Sciliorhinus canicula) are commonly found at the base of the kelp plants around these rugged isolated Atlantic shores.

E - The kelp forests of St.Kilda grow well below 30 metres, since the waters are very clear and unpolluted.

CATHEDRAL ROCK Text by Lawson Wood

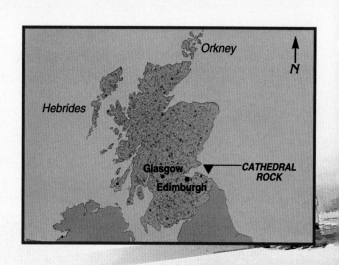

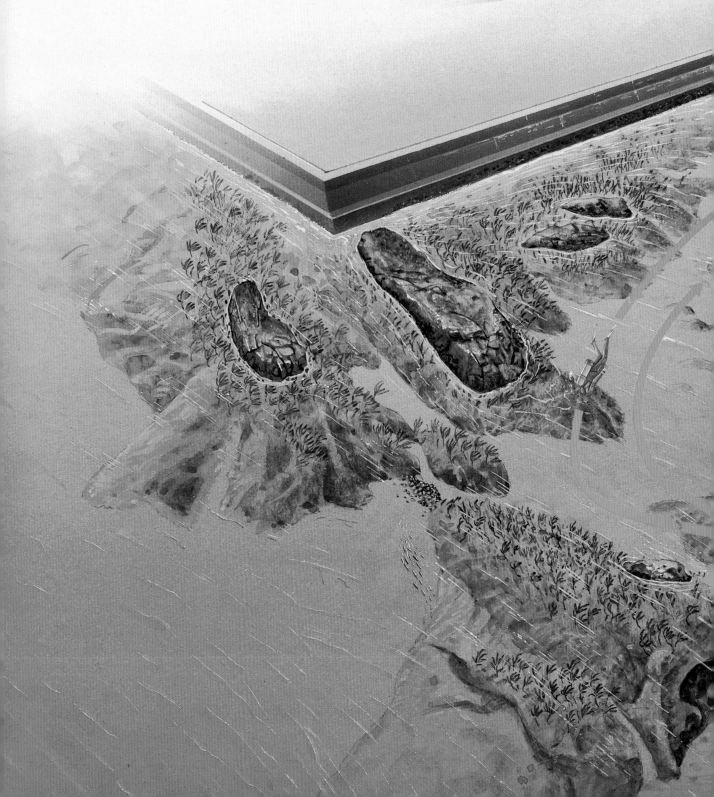

Edimburg

St. Abbs
Eye Mouth

CATHEDRAL
ROCK

N

6 m

8 m

6 m

14 m

6 m

B

C

D

First discovered in the 1950's, Cathedral Rock is the most popular dive site within the St. Abbs and Eyemouth Voluntary Marine Nature Reserve and possibly one of the most dived in the whole of the British Isles. No mean statement, when I first dived the site many years ago, I felt as if I had reached the pinnacle of my diving career and I am sure that even those who also dive this site as their introduction to diving, will agree with me. Cathedral Rock is part of the reef which runs perpendicular to the corner of St. Abbs harbour wall, known locally as Thistley Briggs. The 'rock' of Cathedral Rock is never visible, even at the lowest of tides and many divers mistake the 'rock' for a close-by reef. Underwater, the wall falls away and is deeply undercut with horizontal strata lines eroded away and now filled with squat lobsters and leopard-spotted gobies. The top tunnel is known as the Keyhole and during the diving season, there is often so much trapped air in one of the small upper recesses that you can 'surface' and have a chat whilst still 8 metres underwater.

The lower tunnel archway is massive, of double-decker bus proportions, with a stony bottom directly under the arch and a tumble of boulders at each side. Visibility is variable, depending on the prevailing winds and current, but is generally good. The walls and the roof of the arches are festooned in a dwarf species of the plumose anemone (Metridium senile) as well as sponges, soft corals, mussels and hydroids. Small schools of pollack are often herded into this natural arena by predatory cod.

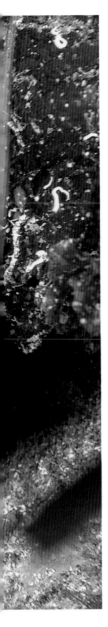

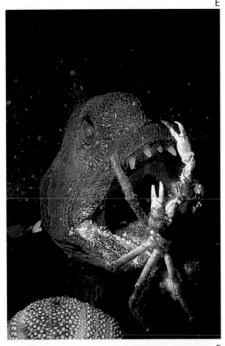

A - A juvenile wolf fish (Anarhichas lupus) peers at the camera from the safety of its fissure in the reef. This species is found only in the northern areas of the region, particularly in Scotland and the coast of Norway.

B - St. Abbs Head is a national nature reserve with many thousands of seabirds nesting on the cliffs. The waters beneath these cliffs provide some of the best diving opportunities in British waters.

C - The gullies and caverns off St.Abbs Head are world-renowned for their clear waters and abundant, varied marine life.

The photographic possibilities of this dive are endless, with panoramic vistas of the archways, diver portraits, diver interaction shots and of course the simply staggering amount of macro work on nudibranchs, crabs and molluscs.

The best access to dive Cathedral Rock is from the southern side of the harbour wall where it joins a low rocky reef. Directly opposite the entry point is another huge rock called Big Green Carr that offers shelter except in the most exceptional of circumstances. Drop down 6 metres onto the small sand and gravel patch smothered in hermit crabs, then swim over to the facing near vertical wall, follow it by keeping it to your left and travel on as far as you can go.

Then cross over a small headland which juts out from the right, swim straight on to the next facing wall which is part of Thistley Briggs and by keeping it to your right you will come to Cathedral Rock - average depth is 8 - 14 metres There is a resident family of Ballan wrasse (Labrus bergylta) which will feed out of the divers' hands.

Divers are nevertheless discouraged to feed the fish with any of the other marine creatures - why kill another animal, just perhaps to get better pictures. Please obey the conservation code, you will be amply rewarded. Due to the position of the rocky reef and two huge holes through it, Cathedral Rock is often swept by current which is funnelled through the archways: although rarely exceeding one knot, this current can still make it a bit of a swim back to the safety of the inner reef. Cathedral Rock is a shore dive. Those of you who are too lazy to swim the 50 metres (165 ft) and take your new RIB to the site, please consider the other divers and snorkellers in the area, as well as the submerged reefs surrounding Cathedral Rock. This site can be dived all year round. As always, however, East coast weather patterns are somewhat variable and diving is liable to be blown out, so remember to telephone any of the dive shops or B&B's well in advance to check on the diving conditions. To get to St. Abbs, travel up the A1 trunk road until you reach Scotland. Turn second right along the Eyemouth to Coldingham road, the A1107. In Coldingham village square, take a tight turning to your right which is well sign-posted to St. Abbs. As you approach the village, the road splits into two.

To get to St.Abbs harbour take the main branch to the right, if you carry straight on, the single track road will pass through Northfield Farm and continues up to St.Abbs lighthouse above the National Nature Reserve. St.Abbs is only about 7 km off the A1. For those of you who have invested in expensive GPS gizmos and insist on diving by boat, Cathedral Rock is at Lat: 550 53' 55"N. Long: 020 07' 29"W.

D - The lesser octopus (Eledone cirrhosa) is actually quite common within the marine reserve and divers see them on most dives, particularly at night.

E -Wolf fish (Anarhichas lupus) are a symbol of the marine reserve and many shore sites have these massive relatives of the common blenny in residence. The wolf fish staple is mainly made up of spider crabs and sea urchins.

F - The walls and roof of Cathedral Rock are covered with plumose anemones (Metridium senile) can be found, extending their feeding polyps into the current to catch planktonic debris.

G - Some of the angler fish reach massive proportions and are unafraid of divers. They use an adapted fin ray as a lure with which to attract unsuspecting prey.

MENAI STRAIT Text by Paul Kay

0 m

14 m

Isles of Anglesey

MENAI STRAIT

Cardigan Bay

NORTH WALES

Lleyn Peninsula
• Criccieth

14 m

A - Approaching the beacon on Swellies Rock in the Strait shows very clearly how strong the currents within the Strait are.

B - Small Spider Crabs cover themselves with sponge so as to blend better against the background of sponge on the seabed.

C - Here Shore Crabs (Carcinus maenas) are feasting on a damaged mussel bank inside the Strait.

D - Many areas of seabed under the Menai Strait are overgrown with sponges of all types and colours.

A

E - Edible Crabs (Cancer pagurus) are abundant within the Strait. They eat many of the barnacles that cover some of the underwater rock surfaces.

F - Many other creatures live on the sponge covering of rocks - here a pretty anemone (Sagartia elegans) and small sea firs.

The Menai Strait separates the Isle of Anglesey from the northern Welsh mainland. In Welsh it is called the Afon Menai which means River Menai. This indicates just how river or estuarine-like it actually looks, partly because of its long narrow appearance, but also because of the strong currents that flow here and give it a very river-like appearance. For many years the Strait has been recognised as a species-rich and special marine area, and has been proposed as a Marine Nature Reserve, a designation that it deserves. Taking a shore-dive at the telegraph cable immediately to the East of the famous Menai Suspension Bridge is by far the easiest and best way to see what the Strait has to offer divers. The site is clearly marked by two yellow diamond-shaped signs, one on each shore. Slack water varies, but starts somewhere between 2 1/2-3 hours before low water at Liverpool. Diving is only possible in slack water. Getting down to the water's edge is simplicity itself. Starting from the Anglesey side, below the suspension bridge (there is a narrow road along the shore, that offers some parking) one must kit up and then walk onto the small grassy green jutting out into the Strait. Narrow steps adjacent to the road wall at the Eastern corner (away from the bridge), lead to a muddy shore. From here it's a matter of following the green to the point where it turns. It is here that the cable is located.

With the cable visible, it is a simple matter of following it! At first it descends slowly over a rock and gravel seabed covered in some seaweed and short kelp. Before long it tumbles much more rapidly down bedrock, and it is here that the Strait really begins to show off its marine life. It is one of the most profuse areas around Britain for sponge growth. Yellow, orange, green and red growths cover everything, be it bedrock, boulder, rubbish or even telegraph cable. The forms that the sponges take vary from simple encrustations through to lumpy masses, finger-like protrusions and long tendrils. It is a strange and eerie undersea world here, for the Strait abounds in water-borne nutrients that encourage the growth of filter feeding animals, like sponges. On the negative side, this results in high turbidity and relatively low visibility! Average visibility is no more than 2-3 m, often less than 1m, and only occasionally exceeds 5m. It has

B

C

been known to extend up to 8m. It was then that the undersea Strait was transformed into a breathtakingly colourful world dominated by an emerald green watery backdrop. Crevices within the sponge provide shelter to many small creatures; crabs, small fish, anemones and sea firs. Few big creatures live in the Strait, the odd lobster or large crab, and perhaps some pollack or bass but otherwise most is small. What they lack in size is made up for in terms of colour and diversity. The Strait also abounds in a wide variety of anemones and seaslugs. Small scorpion spider crabs adorn themselves with sponge in an attempt to disguise their outline and as a

D

consequence make themselves more colourful than usual. But the most prolific creature to be found within the Strait is the shore crab. These are everywhere. They sit breaking off barnacles, trying to open mussels, clasping each other, fighting, and last but not least, trying to hitch a ride from any passing diver! Sometimes they have to be shaken off after a dive - fortunately they too are relatively small. Descending

over the life rich bedrock and boulders finally results in a shingle and gravel plain at around 17m. Here are more creatures - burrowing anemones, scorpion fish, pogges, butterfish and more. It is possible to continue and ascend to the southern shore of the Strait, but access is harder there so the dive is best exited from where it began - a simple matter of turning around and following the cable back. This dive can

be carried out at any time of the year, providing that there is some visibility. Neap tides are best as they give the longest slack, and in winter, one must bear in mind that water temperatures can drop to 3°C! May and June can see significant planktonic blooms which have a decidedly negative effect on visibility!

Despite its murkiness, the Strait is a macro photography paradise. Few diving sites can compete with the Menai Strait in terms of the sheer diversity of its small marine creatures. Slack water lasts for 30 minutes to an hour, and is not enough given the wealth of small subject matter. Backscatter is a problem and careful lighting is required to minimise it. Wide-angle photography is possible but is difficult even in 'good' conditions here, and may require the use of a tripod due to the low available light levels.

Anglesey
Bangor
Caernarfon
CRICCIETH
WALES
Newport
Cardiff
N

10 m

0 m

10 m

A

D

Criccieth lies on the South side of the Lleyn Peninsula in North Wales. It is a pretty little seaside town overlooked by a castle that sits on top of a rounded rocky hill jutting out into the sea. In summer it is a popular holiday destination and, although its beaches are more shingle than sand, it can be quite busy. At first glance it may not appear to offer the diver anything of interest, but this is not so, even if the seabed is largely composed of sand! Essentially Criccieth is a shore dive. It is possible to enter the water just about anywhere along the seafront and swim out into water sufficiently deep to submerge. Entering at either side of, but near the Castle hill is popular. The maximum depth likely to be encountered, even at high tide is less than 10m. Diving here is a matter of swimming southwards as far as is required before turning and heading back. A compass is very useful, although in sunny weather it is possible to navigate using sun and shadows. Little current exists here even during spring tides, so there are no restrictions on diving other than weather. The water here can be quite warm - it often reaches 20C in summer - and visibility is best after a settled spell of gentle northerly or northeasterly winds. Visibility can approach 10m+. Under such conditions it can be very calm with the merest of wavelets lapping the shore, but it is not a viable dive during southerly winds that drastically reduce visibility. At times, after periods of stable calm weather, there can be a considerable build up of bioluminescent plankton in Cardigan Bay. Night dives off Criccieth are easy and safe and with added bioluminescence, become quite ethereal. The seabed off Criccieth is sandy. Most importantly, the sand here is largely undisturbed, being of no interest to trawlers. Although the shore appears to be quite exposed to the South, the shallow sandy seabed appears to be relatively stable - as suggested by the presence of seagrass. Perhaps because of this, the sand seabed here plays host to a

rich and very varied range of underwater life. The site makes for a fascinating dive, especially suited to beginners and inexperienced divers. Any diver with an interest in natural history will find that there is plenty to see on the sand. Some sparse areas of seagrass clumps can be found about 200m off the shore - in Britain, this plant is regarded as being

B

C

nationally scarce. Many creatures find that this plant presents them with an oasis in which to hide. Hermit, delicate long-legged spider and vicious swimming crabs are common around the plants, as are fifteen-spined sticklebacks and greater pipefish. A large number of creatures live directly on the sandy seabed. Partly buried sea-potatoes with their flattened spines. Writhing brittlestars (that can move surprisingly quickly), spiny-edged sandstars, common starfish, shore crabs, various spider crabs, and the like are relatively obvious and quite plentiful. But there are other lesser-known creatures that are more difficult to find. Occasionally little cuttlefish emerge from the sand and jet away from the intruding diver leaving small puffs of black ink as they go. Necklace shellfish and whelks slowly crawl across the sand. Strange masked crabs emerge from the sand and awkwardly scuttle over the seabed. Small flatfish (plaice, flounders, solenette, turbot and the like) dart away.

A - Criccieth's castle is a famous landmark, well known to holidaymakers and visitors to North Wales.

B - A small Hermit Crab (Eupagurus bernhardus) shelters beneath a clump of seagrass at a mere 3 m below the surface

C - One of the strangest creatures seen off Criccieth is the Seamouse (Aphrodite aculeata), actually a scale worm.

D - This male Dragonet (Callionymus lyra) on the sand at a depth of about 5 m, is easily identified by the long first spine on his dorsal fin.

E - Swimming Crabs (Liocarcinus depurator) are common off Criccieth. Many hide by burying themselves, but this one is foraging amongst the seagrass.

F - As the seabed flattens out at the deepest part of the dive pipefish can be seen swimming over a seabed covered with Sand Brittlestars and Sand Mason worms.

G - A Solenette (Buglossidium luteum) illustrates the superb camouflage utilised by some sand dwelling creatures.

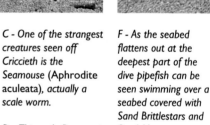

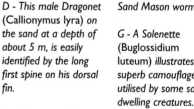

E

F

G

One can even come across a few juvenile rays. Rockling, scorpion fish and many sand gobies can be seen on the sand together with less frequent gurnards and snake pipefish. Semi-transparent anemones live here, such as the Sagartiogeton undatus - not uncommon, but not often seen by divers – with no common name. Strangest of all is the sea mouse, actually a worm but not unlike a land-bound mouse in terms of size and fur! These strange creatures sometimes cruise along the seabed and are easily identifiable by their size, shape and the iridescent fur along their sides. As the whole area is shallow, long dives can be undertaken here. It is an area for pottering and simply watching the undersea world. Life in all its facets goes on here, irrespective of whether a diver has intruded, and makes fascinating viewing. In warm summer conditions, the seabed can be well lit providing for good visibility and a very pleasant dive. Criccieth is a wonderful dive for the photographer. It is a macro world out on the sand with subjects ranging from hand to fingernail in size. The wealth of subject matter is surprising, especially since a lot of it is only found on sand, a relatively unusual backdrop for most underwater photographers. Action photography is available from darting little cuttlefish and shrimps that bury themselves very quickly indeed. Watch out for the lesser weever fish that can literally disappear under the sand. This fish has poisonous spines that can cause very painful stings. Since it is quite common here, it may be a good idea to wear protective gloves. Weevers are very difficult to photograph!

MANACLES Text by Mark Webster

0 m

3 m

8 m

35 m

48 m

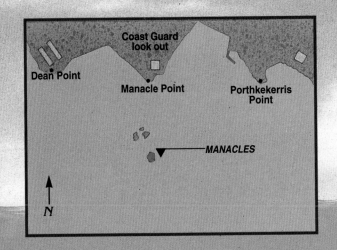

Dean Point

Coast Guard
look out

Manacle Point

Porthkekerris
Point

MANACLES

N

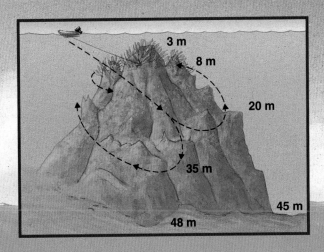

3 m

8 m

20 m

35 m

45 m

48 m

W

S

N

E

A

The land mass of the Lizard peninsula is the southernmost point of the United Kingdom. Its position reaching out into the English Channel has been a major navigational landmark as well as a hazard since the earliest days of sailing. The granite cliffs, sheltered bays and offshore reefs boast some of the best diving that this area has to offer. One of the most popular of these areas is the infamous Manacles reef which lies on the north eastern side of the peninsula at the edge of Falmouth Bay. This reef comprises a series of granite peaks and ledges rising sharply from depths of 60-70m to break the surface or lurk just 2m or 3m below the water.

Many ships have met their fate here perhaps travelling to or from the port of Falmouth or simply hugging the coastline too closely when making for the Lizard peninsula.

This reef area rates as probably the most spectacular in Falmouth Bay, but must

only be dived when the conditions are right. Vicious tides of up to 5 knots are experienced here, and the current continues to run sometimes even during 'slack' periods on a spring tide, and sadly there have been several diving tragedies in the area. The best diving is found on the outer reefs of the Manacles where the reefs are most exposed to the tide and the density of marine life is often quite staggering. Much of the reef system is not surface breaking, so it is important to go with a boatman who knows the area and tides and has the right equipment to identify the sites. The whole area offers potentially excellent diving, so if you do visit, try more than one of the reefs as they all have a different feel and topography.

Raglans Reef is the most seaward of the reefs and looks very impressive on the echo sounder rising sheer from a depth of 50-60m like a church spire to within 3-4m of the surface. The reef can only be located with a combination of landmarks

B

and transits or a GPS fix and an echo sounder. You should plan your dive for slack water and preferably on a neap tide for a long dive. Arriving on location before the tide is slack will enable you to spot the surface disturbance caused by the tidal waters being thrown towards the surface by the obstruction of the reef. This will give a clue to the location of the reef top and you may begin your sweep with the echo sounder upstream of the disturbance. When you are waiting for the tide to stop running there will often be a 'false slack' period when the current appears to stop only to

C

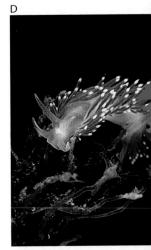

D

E

restart again with a final surge 10 or 15 minutes later. It is possible to dive at this moment when there is a neap tide, but on a spring it is best to wait for full slack water. If you are experienced then it is possible to start or finish your dive when the tide is running as the reef will offer shelter on one side. However, your boatman must be experienced and remain alert to the possibility of divers being carried away by the tide particularly at the end of a dive. Always carry a surface marker buoy here so that your boat can spot you easily on the surface. The other cautionary note for this area is its popularity especially on holiday weekends when there will be a large number of diving boats operating in the area. So be aware of other boat traffic especially when surfacing at the end of a dive away from the reef.

To be certain of locating the reef when you leave the surface it is best for the boat to anchor to the reef top or to deploy a marker buoy on a grapnel or shot weight. If you miss the narrow reef top then you run the risk of not finding the reef at all or hitting it at a depth far greater than planned. The top 5-8m has a heavy growth of kelp with widely spaced stypes which provides shelter for many marine organisms. This area is best left for exploration until the end of your dive when you are decompressing or making a safety stop. Just below the kelp line around 8m the rocks are covered with hydroids, masses of brittle stars, endless arrays of jewel anemones and soft corals. The best route to follow is to

start on the north east side of the pinnacle where you will find a series of vertical rock faces which are carpeted with sea fans and plumose anemones in a variety of colours. Follow these to your target depth but bear in mind that you can easily find yourself in 45m to 50m depth before you see the surrounding seabed. From this point you can begin to swim around the pinnacle either west or east dependent on which way any current may be flowing. On the reef edge watch out for shoals of bass which like to congregate in the eddies created by the current striking the rock faces and feed off the disturbed plankton . As you make your way around towards the south face gradually decreasing your depth, you will find that the sheer rock faces change to a series of large ledges and boulders with small sandy patches collected in the hollows. Stop and inspect these as you will often find angler fish, topknot flat fish or dog fish and tope resting here. The decreasing depth will also reveal more reef fish activity with ballan wrasse, goldsinney wrasse and the very bold and inquisitive cuckoo wrasse approaching you to investigate this odd visitor. In the spring there will be clouds of juvenile fish shoaling just below the kelp line often being herded and hunted by marauding groups of pollack some of which reach an impressive size and are very bold. This is an excellent site for photography, not least due to the range of subjects, but also because of the depth ranges available in one dive - go deep first, then decompress in the shallows looking for macro subjects. The simplest method of finding Raglans reef is to use the set of three transits shown in the accompanying sketch together with an echo sounder. Start your search some 2-300m seaward of the Voices rocks which are the southernmost rocks breaking the surface at most states of the tide. Line the southern side of the rocks with the two conveyor chutes at the quarry on Dean Point. The second mark is on the north side of the Voices lined up with the coast guard hut on Manacle Point. The third is the headland of Pencra Head just covering the small Ministry of Defence building on the north side of Porthkerris cove. The charted position of Raglans Reef is 50°02'63"N, 05°02'45"W. Slack water is generally found one hour before low water and one hour after high water at Falmouth.

A - On the sandy shelves in the reef wall you will often encounter angler fish (Lophius piscatorius) lying in wait for an easy meal. Some grow to huge proportions and will allow you to come close, if you're careful not to alarm them.

B – Exploring the shallows at the top of the reef in early spring will often lead to an encounter with the strange looking lump sucker (Cyclopterus lumpus).

C – A group of plumose anemones (Metridium senile) reach into the nutrient rich current to feed just below the kelp line at the top of the reef.

D - The Oaten pipe hydroids (Tubularia indivisa) are common all over the reef and are the preferred food of the attractive Flabellina nudibranch (Coryphella browni). This species ingests the stinging cells of the hydroid and transfers them to the tips of the cerata on its back for use as defence against predators.

E - The striking looking John Dory (Zeus faber) slips between the kelp stypes as it hunts. This fish is very difficult to spot head on as it has such a slim profile. You must wait for the fish to turn when it will be seen easily.

PORTHKERRIS COVE
Text by Mark karries

Helford River

N

Lizard Peninsula

Porthallow

Porthkerris

PORTHKERRIS
COVE

St. Keverne

N

25 m

75 m

15 m

150 m

6 m

100 m

A - *Delicate sea squirts* (Phallusia mammillata) *are found in sheltered parts of the reef. This one has attracted a juvenile starfish which is feeding on the algae coating the stem of the sea squirt.*

B - *Snake pipe fish* (Entelurus aequoreus) *are common in the shallows but are very difficult to spot. You must patiently search amongst the kelp and seaweed where they hang vertically motionless for much of the time.*

C

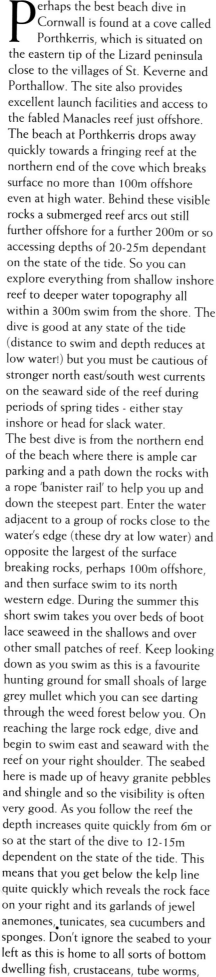

A

B

Perhaps the best beach dive in Cornwall is found at a cove called Porthkerris, which is situated on the eastern tip of the Lizard peninsula close to the villages of St. Keverne and Porthallow. The site also provides excellent launch facilities and access to the fabled Manacles reef just offshore. The beach at Porthkerris drops away quickly towards a fringing reef at the northern end of the cove which breaks surface no more than 100m offshore even at high water. Behind these visible rocks a submerged reef arcs out still further offshore for a further 200m or so accessing depths of 20-25m dependant on the state of the tide. So you can explore everything from shallow inshore reef to deeper water topography all within a 300m swim from the shore. The dive is good at any state of the tide (distance to swim and depth reduces at low water!) but you must be cautious of stronger north east/south west currents on the seaward side of the reef during periods of spring tides - either stay inshore or head for slack water.

The best dive is from the northern end of the beach where there is ample car parking and a path down the rocks with a rope 'banister rail' to help you up and down the steepest part. Enter the water adjacent to a group of rocks close to the water's edge (these dry at low water) and opposite the largest of the surface breaking rocks, perhaps 100m offshore, and then surface swim to its north western edge. During the summer this short swim takes you over beds of boot lace seaweed in the shallows and over other small patches of reef. Keep looking down as you swim as this is a favourite hunting ground for small shoals of large grey mullet which you can see darting through the weed forest below you. On reaching the large rock edge, dive and begin to swim east and seaward with the reef on your right shoulder. The seabed here is made up of heavy granite pebbles and shingle and so the visibility is often very good. As you follow the reef the depth increases quite quickly from 6m or so at the start of the dive to 12-15m dependent on the state of the tide. This means that you get below the kelp line quite quickly which reveals the rock face on your right and its garlands of jewel anemones, tunicates, sea cucumbers and sponges. Don't ignore the seabed to your left as this is home to all sorts of bottom dwelling fish, crustaceans, tube worms, anemones and in the spring and summer

months hordes of juvenile cuttlefish. The reef is dissected by a number of cuts and gullies all crying out to be explored, but your first dive here is best spent generally familiarising yourself with the topography and routing for your return. So, continue seaward until the large reef wall terminates on your right and you encounter some large individual rocks which is the beginning of the reef running further out into deeper water. Here, depending on the tide, you can either continue seaward on the low reef to deeper water and return along the same route, or continue right along the 'back' southern face of the reef. Along this back wall of the reef there is a section of wall, slightly undercut in places, which reaches 4-5m in height before the reef forms a series of steps and ledges towards the surface. Because this face is exposed to tidal current it is covered with filter feeding dead men's fingers (soft corals), jewel anemones and sponges which makes it quite colourful especially in the beam of a torch. The maximum depth here approaches 18-19m at high water and this area is home to several varieties of fish such as marauding pollack and the occasional bass, ballan and corkwing wrasse, cheeky cuckoo wrasse who peer right into your mask and more unusual species such as red gurnard and john dory's. Following this wall south you will come to the end of the first main 'block' of reef and the reef becomes more dissected and broken, though no less massive. This area offers all sorts of gullies and undercuts to be explored and you can happily work your way along this area

until the reef begins to rise on your right towards the gully between two rocks. Either follow the gully or continue around one of the two rocks towards the shore once more. From here you can either follow the patches of rock and reef on the seabed on a compass bearing towards the shore (easiest if there is any tide) or surface and swim back.

Once you have explored this largest section of reef you can try the alternative of swimming north at the beginning of the dive towards the smaller submerged reef shown in the diagram. These rocks are also swept by the current and so have their own cloak of soft corals and anemones. In the summer months you will find this a good spot to watch corkwing wrasse nest building and you will often find blond rays and cuttle fish buried in the sand. On the furthest rock are several large lobsters who so far have survived the interest of visiting divers, so please just record them on film.

If you choose to follow the reef seaward choose a slack water period and ensure you have a good compass bearing for your return and enough air for the swim. The reef gently peters out in 25m or so on a dark sandy seabed where there is a healthy scallop bed. Even on a neap tide the current out here can be quite strong as you are beyond the shelter of the headland, so be cautious and turn back with plenty of air as a surface swim can be extremely hard work!

If you make the swim offshore do be wary of departing and returning boats either from the dive centre or visiting

groups and clubs. The Manacles are a mere 15 minutes away and the wreck of the Volnay just a ten-minute boat ride, so when it is busy these boats run a shuttle service to and from the dive sites. Also, don't be too surprised if you meet something bigger than yourself out in the bay during the summer months. Basking sharks can be seen in within 100m of the beach and pods of dolphins.

The cove nestles under high cliffs and is protected from most winds except those from the east. So in the summer, when the prevailing winds are occasionally very strong from the south west, Porthkerris is generally flat calm. Since the establishment of the dive centre here the cove has grown in popularity although it is rarely crowded except on bank holiday weekends. It is an ideal base for a club holiday with the tremendous variety of diving on hand for novice and experienced divers alike and offers excellent facilities.

RUNNEL STONE Text by Mark Webster

0 m

5 m

10 m

20 m

30 m

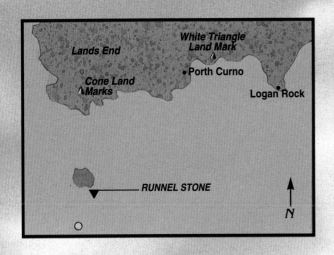

Lands End

White Triangle
Land Mark

Cone Land
Marks

Porth Curno

Logan Rock

RUNNEL STONE

N

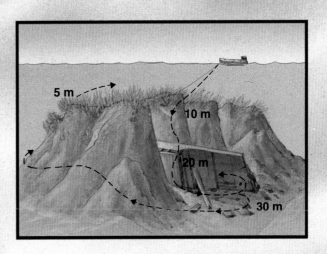

5 m

10 m

20 m

30 m

Close to Land's End is the infamous Runnel Stone which is reputed to have wrecked more than 27 ships. The Runnel Stone is in fact an extensive area of reefs and pinnacles which lost its only surface breaking feature to the last vessel to be wrecked on the Stone, the City of Westminster in 1923. The reef is now marked by a buoy within sight of Land's End and the Longships reef lighthouse and is consequently open to Atlantic oceanic conditions.

The topography is immensely rugged, the geology granite and serpentine, which produces a bright yellow heavy sand, and there are no river out-falls to upset visibility. This whole area provides a rich microcosm of reef life in temperate waters.

Due to the strong currents at this location only the hardiest of sea weeds are able to take hold and thrive. However, the kelp canopy here extends down to between 5 and 8 metres, less where the reef walls are particularly sheer, and provides shelter for a wide variety of marine life both sedentary and mobile. Sponges abound and the first signs of jewel and daisy anemones can be found in as little as 3 metres of water. Looking up towards the kelp line graceful plumose anemones can be seen extended sifting the current. In amongst them are daisy and dahlia anemones. Where the kelp ends, the fields of jewel anemones begin in almost every colour you can imagine from vivid yellows to deep purples. These are interspersed with the stems of hydroids reaching out to feed. Remaining space on the rock

A

B

surface is occupied by masses of feather stars and brittle stars again seemingly in every hue on a painter's palette.

Along the wall you will find countless nooks, crannies and ledges which are home to crabs, squat lobsters, blennies, shannies and prawns most of which are both inquisitive and co-operative. You should keep your eyes open for scorpion fish and the Corkwing wrasse which can be found busy building its nest early in the summer. Cowries and topshells are common on the kelp holdfasts and there is normally an abundance of spider crabs picking their way amongst the kelp stypes. Look carefully at the stypes as you will often be lucky enough to see more than one pipefish taking advantage of their camouflage. As you go deeper the reef system offers walls, gullies and plateaux which support an astounding wealth of marine life, even playing host to occasional sub-tropical visitors such as triggerfish and sunfish. It is common to encounter large shoals of mackerel, bass and pollock which show little fear of divers. Amongst the rocks you will find the remains of the numerous wrecks, which in some cases are so close or overlapping that it is difficult to tell when you swim from one to another. One of the best known and the largest is the City of Westminster which now lies on the south side of the Stone. She was on a voyage in October 1923 from Belfast to Rotterdam with a cargo of 2400 tons of maize when she ran into dense banks of fog as she rounded Land's End. In those days the top of the Runnel broke

the surface and was marked by a beacon, but this was entirely invisible to the skipper in these conditions. The ship was too close inshore and she hit the stone under full power, so hard that the bows broke off the top 3-5m of the stone complete with the beacon as the hull drove over the reef ripping out her keel. The ship quickly broke her back and disappeared beneath the waves, fortunately without any loss of life. Her remains include the bows and mid-ship section at 20-25m whilst her stern lies a little off the main reef at 50-55m below the surface and is consequently rarely dived. The ship is well broken open by the pounding of the Atlantic swells here, but there are many recognisable features and if you search in the gullies on the north face of the reef you will even find the remains of the Runnel Stone beacon. It is possible to satisfy

C

every diver's taste on the Runnel Stone with more wreckage than you could sensibly cope with and the option and contrast of the adjacent spectacular drop-offs and gullies for photographers and marine life observers. Visibility here is generally very good, and visibility of 20m is not uncommon, although the plankton bloom in late spring/early summer will reduce this but will bring the possibility of an encounter with a massive basking shark or squadrons of huge Rhysostoma jelly fish.

The best period of slack water is one and a half hours before low tide at Penzance, although it is possible to dive on a high water slack during neap tides. No site along this stretch of coast should be dived without the benefit of local knowledge which is best sourced from the local diving clubs or charter boats. If you are diving from your own

boat then the Runnel Stone is easy to find using landmarks and an echo sounder. Position your boat close to the buoy and look towards the shore at Land's End. On the cliff top you will see two cones, the closest one red and one further inshore, which is black and white. Line these two up as you steam slowly inshore from the buoy whilst looking north east towards the headland (Ped-men-an-mere) adjacent to the cliff top Minack theatre and the cove of Porth Curno. On the cliff top on the far side of Porth Curno is a white triangular land mark, as this begins to be covered by the headland you will be over the Runnel Stone. Watch your echo sounder as the depth jumps from 35-40m to 5-6m perhaps 150-200m from the buoy (see sketch). The charted position of the stone is 50°1'33"N, 5°40'33"W.

D

A - The top of the Runnel Stone reef is dissected by deep gullies carpeted by anemones.

B - In early spring you will often encounter the strange looking lump sucker (Cyclopterus lumpus) guarding its eggs amongst the kelp stypes.

C - Delicate Oaten pipe hydroids (Tubularia indivisa) cover many of the rock surfaces where they reach into the current to feed.

D - These gaudily coloured dahlia anemones (Urticina felina), which grow in great swathes, give the reef an almost tropical feel.

WORM HOLE Text by Paul Kay

N

Galway

Rossaveel

Inish Mór

Aran
Islands

WORM HOLE

12 m

10 m

25 m

A - The true dimensions of the Worm Hole can only be fully appreciated when an appropriate scale - such as a diver - is seen within it..

B - Dense kelp forest appears impenetrable but merely cloaks some excellent diving outside the Worm Hole.

C - The Worm Hole appears as a natural swimming pool when viewed from the clifftop.

Inish Mór is the largest of the three Aran Isles that lie in the entrance to Galway Bay. It is composed of limestone that weathers easily and gives rise to some curious rocky formations both above and below the surface. The Worm Hole itself is an extremely unusual geological formation. It is basically a natural cavity in the sloping limestone bedrock shore about the size, shape and regularity of a good-sized swimming pool. It is filled with seawater, and whilst it is not obvious from a landward viewing, the Hole is connected to the sea by an underground tunnel. The Irish name for the Worm Hole is Poll na bPéist of which the 'peist' refers to a mythological reptilian monster. Whilst it is easy to see why such folklore should have come into being, the Worm Hole is famous today not for its sea monsters, but rather for its spectacular undersea access. The Worm Hole is a boat dive requiring quite a lengthy journey from either the mainland or one of the Aran Islands. Good weather is an essential precondition for diving the Worm Hole - anything stronger than a force three wind makes the entrance inaccessible because of the waves breaking on the rocks above it. In bad weather the waves which lash this coast are oceanic,

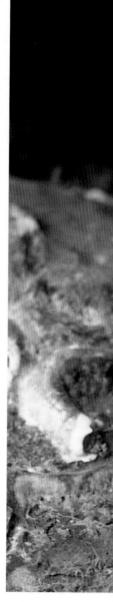

from the open Atlantic, and are incredibly powerful. In good weather the same water is blue in colour and but for its temperature (rarely above 13°C), could easily be tropical. To see the Worm Hole in its full glory clear water is a must - fortunately the west coast of Ireland can and does have visibility exceeding 30 m at times and this is when the dive is at its best.

Given good visibility, blue-skies and flat calm seas, the Worm Hole is a world class dive. In the right conditions, diving the Worm Hole is easy enough. A good boat handler will manoeuvre close to the coast outside the Worm Hole, and drop divers within 20-30 m from the shore. From here it is a simple matter of working in towards the rock, then down to about 10-12 m when the tunnel should become quite obvious. Whilst there is some life in the tunnel, especially encrusting creatures like coral worms, in essence the dive is spectacular in terms of its scenery. From inside the tunnel, which is boulder strewn, the Worm Hole may be seen in totality from below. If the weather is sunny, then streams of light filter through the water producing a magical effect and giving this natural pool an enchanting air. Some kelp lines the pool both along its sides and its seabed, and smaller red seaweed also covers many rock surfaces injecting colour into the shallow scene. On the right hand side, at the base of the rock, are crevices, that are home to large tompot blennies and crabs. Surfacing reinforces the regularity of this rocky feature, and many have wondered whether it was actually the result of man's efforts - it is

D - Many colourful Painted Topshells (Calliostoma zizyphinum) can be found amongst the encrusting life on the tunnel and cave walls around the Wormhole..

E - Shy Wrasse make elusive subjects for video or still cameras, but are abundant enough to make the trouble well worth one's while.

F - Velvet Swimming Crabs (Liocarcinus puber) are abundant within the numerous crevices found in the bedrock coast.

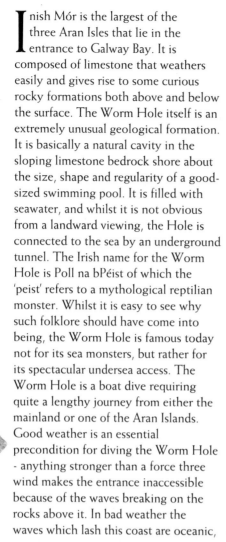

A

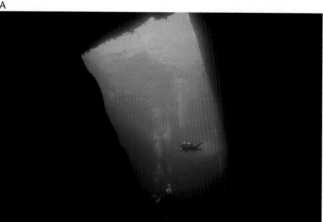

B

E

F

completely natural though.
The pool's sheltered water and quietness contrast strongly with the open coast just a few metres away! Descending again and exiting through the tunnel, brings an open coastal area into view.

Initially off-putting, extensive kelp forest covers the rock, but it is well worth finning through this, as to the left of the entrance (as you view it from the sea) lies a cave. Whilst not very extensive, it is large enough to require a good torch and is full of Devonshire

cup corals and a myriad of squat lobsters. The sides of the cave are deeply fissured with crevices, in the larger of which it is possible to spot an occasional common lobster or spiny spider crab. Many crawfish live here and it is not unusual to see one or more in the cave or around its entrance. The cave's sides are also coated with numerous small encrusting organisms and are multicoloured and fascinating to look at in close-up. After finishing in the cave, if air and time allows, it is still worth finning further out, away from

the cliff, for here the kelp lies on top of massive boulders, some in excess of 10 m in diameter. Many are perched on small bedrock pinnacles and it is possible to swim beneath some and explore the cavities and tunnels so created. Wrasse are common here with many ballan and rock cook curious to see what divers are doing in this relatively infrequently dived part of the sea.

This really is wide-angle country! In the best conditions there are superb photo opportunities within the Worm Hole especially if a diver is placed in the picture to lend a scale; even without help like this the Worm Hole can produce spectacular images. Outside is still very good with a wide-angle although within the cave you may require a macro. The fish in the open sea are somewhat shy and so you may require a longer macro lens to capture them effectively.

BRANNOCK ISLAND Text by Paul Kay

10 m

20 m

30 m

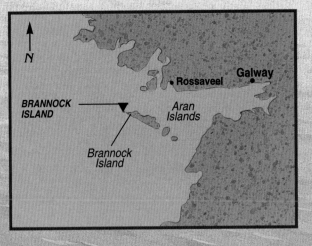

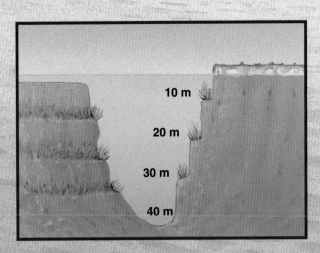

A - A large number of Dead Men's Fingers (Alcyonium digitatum) adorn the bedrock below the luxuriant kelp forest

B - The delicate Actinothöe sphyrodeta is an anemone commonly found around Brannock Island.

C - Abundant subject matter (here a crevice) makes the area one of great interest to underwater videographers.

C

D

F - Vast numbers of vividly coloured Jewel Anemones (Corynactis viridis) coat most vertical rock surfaces.

G - The unmistakable male Cuckoo wrasse is a common and inquisitve fish found in good numbers around Brannock.

H - Whilst not generally found at Brannock Island, the large Fireworks Anemone (Pachycerianthus multiplicatus) is just one of the many unusual creatures recently sighted in the area.

Channel Location Brannock Island is a small island on the Channel, just to the West of the westernmost point of Aran Island, Inish Mór. It is separated by a narrow but deep channel. This channel is divided into a series of steps produced by the weathering of layers of limestone. These steps are irregular, have some very steep faces, some overhangs, many fissures and cracks and in places are intersected by deep, narrow gullies. As water sweeps through the channel, many species characteristic of such areas are to be found here. With visibility generally very good here (it can exceed 30m) the dive is beautiful both in terms of its scenery and the marine life found here.

The whole area of the channel is varied. The best way to dive the channel is to drop in on the Inish Mór side in

A

B

D - The colour of anemones and sponges is as brilliant as that found in warmer waters.

E - Limestone bedrock provides many crevices where Crawfish (Palinurus elaphas) can be found.

E

relatively shallow water (around 5-10m). The use of a sounder makes this quite a straightforward operation, and upon entering the water the kelp covered reeftop should be clearly visible). It is then best to descend over the steps to the maximum desired depth, before working slowly up and along. The steps vary considerably in width and in depth.

Some slope whilst other just peter out into vertical cliffs. Many of the horizontal planes extend back into the vertical cliff faces, undercutting them and forming shallow overhang caves (or more properly cavities). These are lined with encrusting life including many thousands of jewel anemones, as are many of the shorter overhangs found at the top edge of many vertical faces. Sometimes ross or rose coral colonies can be seen although these are far from common.

The colour of the jewel anemones and myriad dead men's fingers can be quite startling. Amidst these are urchins, plumose anemones and occasional white seafans. There is a tremendous amount of encrusting life plastered onto the cliff walls, Sagartia anemones, Actinothöe anemones, various seasquirts, and many other encrusting organisms. Fish too are abundant. Wrasse, especially cuckoo - both male and female - are curious, but keep their distance. Large ballan wrasse peer at divers until spotted whereupon the dart away in embarrassment. Pollack too move around in shoals, some quite large. In the crevices scorpion fish lie still relying upon their indistinct outline and varied colours to blend them into the cacophony of colour already there. Add to these the crawfish and a variety of crabs and it is obvious that the whole dive is full of creatures to look at. The undersea scenery too is spectacular. It is possible to fin along a ledge and to see the next ten or fifteen meters below, whilst kelp fronds sway rhythmically over the clifftop above. As the ledges curve around, there is always a new scene around the next corner, where perhaps a ledge has fallen away leaving a huge deep gully between it and the resulting cliff-face.

The scenery of this dive depends very much on which ledge is followed, or whether different ledges are explored. When visibility is good and the weather is fair, the whole area is quite delightful, even in the shallow regions that are densely overgrown with kelp. The constant swaying of the kelp can be surprisingly soothing. A word of caution, however. This area is extensively fished, so the use of delayed action surface marker buoys is desirable just prior to surfacing so that no boat is too close. It should also be noted that it is illegal for divers to take any form of shellfish in Irish waters!

The biggest problem is which lens to take! This is an excellent dive for both wide-angle or macro and has fish a-plenty too. Visibility can be superb and when it is, the site simply cries out to be covered by a wide-angle. At the same time, a wide-angle lens would not do justice to the stunning array of colourful marine life here. Perhaps the best advice is to take two cameras, if at all possible!

G

H

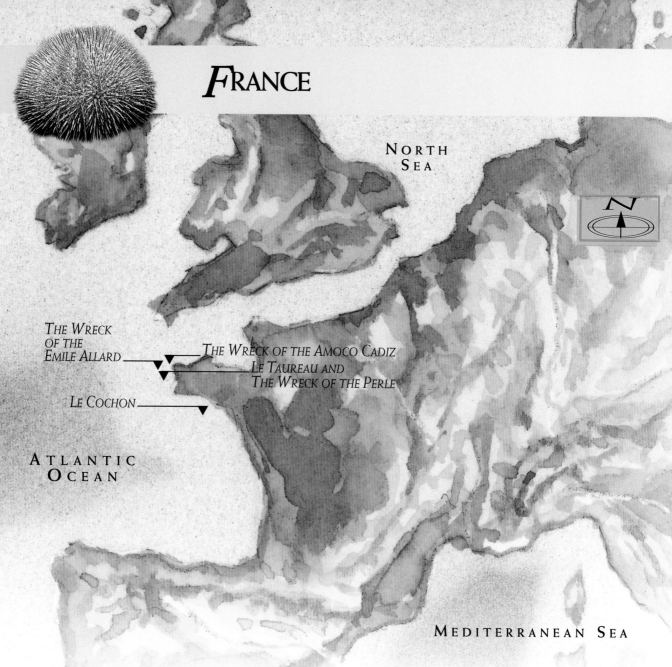

FRANCE

NORTH
SEA

THE WRECK
OF THE
EMILE ALLARD

THE WRECK OF THE AMOCO CADIZ
LE TAUREAU AND
THE WRECK OF THE PERLE

LE COCHON

ATLANTIC
OCEAN

MEDITERRANEAN SEA

A

Between St. Malo in the North and St. Nazaire in the South, Brittany boasts a good thousand kilometres of coastline, opening on to the English Channel and the Atlantic Ocean. The coastline is very irregular, featuring capes and bays with extensive carpets of rock off the coast, isolated rocky masses, as well as a large number of islands and islets, with scores of wrecks located at various depths thrown in for good measure. All this is steeped in waters of exceptional marine wealth, with flora and fauna of almost unimaginable variety, providing an incalculable number of underwater sites, suited to all tastes and all levels of diving skill. A word of caution however: these are ocean waters and diving here entails a certain number of precautions that every diver must be fully familiar with, before getting into the water. The climate in

Brittany has little in common with the Mediterranean clime. Temperate and humid, Breton weather is permanently at the mercy of the whims of the Atlantic. Before any diving expedition, therefore, one must always consult the weatherman, who may announce the arrival of areas of low pressure, harbingers of bad weather off the coast. While news of imminent pockets of low pressure in Brittany is always available sufficiently beforehand, unexpected depressions are not entirely unknown. This demands constant vigilance by divers even if one has no plans to venture far from the coast. It is also important to bear in mind that differences between high and low tides can often reach seven metres at Brest. These tidal differences have enormous impact on the underwater landscape as certain rocks visible from the surface at low tide may be totally submerged at

B

A - The French Atlantic coast is frequently ravaged by severe storms that cause a large number of shipwrecks. Many wrecks become splendid diving sites, such as the wreck of the Amoco Cadiz.

B - The rocky plateaux are sometimes covered by forests of Himanthalia that rise to several metres.

undertaken with one or two reliable underwater torches fitted with new batteries. Lastly, still on the subject of equipment, since the mean underwater temperature in Brittany varies between 8 and 16 degrees, a thick wetsuit should be used, complete with booties and gloves, or even better, a variable volume diving suit. If all these precautions are meticulously followed, diving in this region will open the door to an extraordinary world, teeming with a fantastic diversity of underwater fauna such as, wrasses, conger-eels, flatfish, whiting-pouts, saithes, sea-basses, crustaceans, etc. … Brittany also offers a vast variety of fixed marine creatures in a wide range of colours that fascinate the eye under torchlight. Each wreck is a world unto itself, just waiting to be discovered. However, precautions must be doubled when visiting wrecks. One last point – when diving in Brittany, divers are well advised to make life

high tide. Tidal differences are calculated on the basis of a scale, whose maximum value is 120. These values are indicated, together with times of high and low tide on a tidal almanac that every diver would be well advised to obtain and consult regularly. When diving in Brittany, one has to deal with currents, that are closely linked with the tides. The strength of currents varies according to the extent of tidal differences. Diving is best undertaken in slack water (when the current is reversed) and at the lowest possible tides.

Diving in Brittany also entails another major concern: safety. While it is common sense that no diver should ever venture out alone, not all divers take the added precaution of having a well-secured anchor line and efficient surface assistance. All divers must always carry a signal mirror, a whistle, and if possible, emergency flares packed in a watertight sheath, so as to signal their location, should they be carried away by the current. It goes without saying that any exploration of wrecks must be

C - The Atlantic coast teems with thousands of crustaceans. Spider crabs (Maja squinado) congregate in shallow water here, to mate in the spring.

D - Amongst the large number of invertebrates anchored to the rocks, yellow alcyonarians (Alcyonium digitatum) are found together with black ophiuroids (Ophiocomina nigra).

C

D

easier and to avoid risks by utilising the services of a diving centre, that will only be too happy to provide access to a particular isolated rock or to a wreck, covered by alcyonarians, in the safest and therefore the most enjoyable conditions.

THE WRECK OF THE AMOCO CADIZ
Text by Patrick Mouton

0 m

5 m

30 m

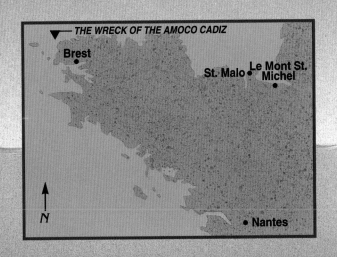

THE WRECK OF THE AMOCO CADIZ

Brest

St. Malo • Le Mont St.
Michel

N

• Nantes

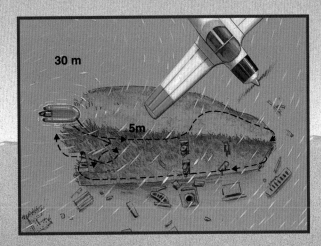

30 m

5m

A - The granite cliffs of the Atlantic coast continue underwater in the forms of huge heaps of rock that feature countless cracks, fissures and caves.

B - The ship's stern, lying at a depth of 25 metres, still supports its lantern mast.

On March 16, 1978, in very bad weather, the supertanker *Amoco Cadiz* fell victim to a rudder malfunction off the coast of Finistere. Despite all the efforts by emergency tugs, the gigantic 300 metre long vessel drifted in the huge labyrinth of the shallows of Portsall, to the North of Brest, before running aground against what can only be described as a rocky carpet. Her bow then rose above the water while the rest of the vessel gradually sank, spewing 230,000 tons of crude oil to create one of the largest oil spills in history. Today, her stem that broke off and drifted away has disappeared. Now one knows where it rests. Her huge hull lies at a depth of 30 metres, nearly completely dismembered by violent currents, savage western winds and the dynamite charges of French naval divers. Only her stern remains relatively well preserved. All the rest is nothing more than a heap of more or less large shapeless and dismembered pieces of sheet iron, scattered by the waves. Because of her distance from the coast and the strong currents, it is highly advisable to consult the diving centre that is very familiar with the area and that provides excellent surface safety. At any rate, diving is only possible during slack water. But a visit to the *Amoco* is a unique experience of its kind, exuding a sort of charm, not least because of the terrible history of this giant vessel and the ecological disaster her sinking entailed. Three centres are equipped to conduct perfectly safe diving expeditions: The Landunvez Diving Centre, Argenton port, 29840 Landunvez; l'Aber Benoit Plongée, quai du Stellac'h, BP 68, Saint Pabu; le Centre Aber Sub, Port de l'Aberwrac'h, 2970 Landeda.
Once the diving party reaches the site, it is wise to first send a diver to secure the anchor line to the highest part of the

wreck, between five and seven metres below the surface, depending on the tide. The stern of the tanker is quite steeply inclined on her port side. After reaching the highest pieces of sheet metal, one should go along the vessel's starboard side towards the stern, taking care to avoid the handrail stanchions that are hidden amongst seaweed and that are dangerous to touch. At the stern, the ship's name *Amoco Cadiz* is still clearly legible on her hull. Under the stern, at a depth of 30 metres, one can see the rudder, half buried in the sand. It is at this point that the sheer size of the vessel really hits the onlooker. After having visited the stern, one should proceed towards the bow by going along the port side of the hulk, so as to see the huge bitts and windlasses still intact on the stern. At the point where the hull is broken, one can go into the hold, using one or two lamps to enter an extraordinary, oversized environment and to see the stem of the rudder. On leaving, one should proceed towards the left, until one gets back to the anchor line attached to the upper parts of the wreck. While underwater life around the *Amoco Cadiz* is not as abundant as around other wrecks in Brittany, one can still come across schools of whiting-

C - Care must be taken to avoid getting lost in the confusion of sheet metal of the wreck, that stretch for 200 metres along the seabed.

D - At a depth of 20 metres, on the starboard side of the stern, one leaves the bridge covered by laminaria. By scratching the surface of the hull, one can easily read the ship's name.

pouts, small crabs, and 'dog teeth' madrepores, that have colonised a large part of the after tank. Given the size of the wreck, several dives may be undertaken here, always however, strictly respecting the basic diving safety rules applicable to all of Brittany: one must always ensure that the weather is stably calm, diving must only be undertaken at slack water, excellent surface assistance services must be constantly available and high quality underwater torches must be used.

E - The after deck was fitted with two huge winches still visible, under the laminaria.

F - The huge engine room has collapsed, but other parts of the ship remain to be explored.

G - Under the after deck, the steering drag link compartment (that caused the disaster), is the only really intact area of the ship.

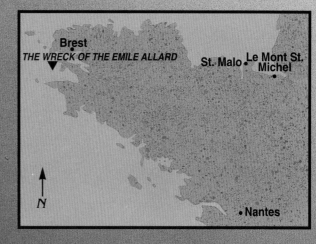

THE WRECK OF THE EMILE ALLARD

Text by Patrick Mouton

25 m

N

19 m

22 m

28 m

A

B

C

D

Forty-seven metres in length and with a net tonnage of 204 tons, this small vessel was launched at Le Havre in 1933. Equipped to maintain the large number of lighthouses and the hundreds of beacons that dot the coast of Brittany, she is easily recognisable because of her stem supporting two large horns and the lifting crane installed on her bow to place and remove buoys. In 1940, with her entire crew, she escaped from the Dunkirk pocket and tried to reach England, where ... she was turned back and forced to return to France! The following year, she was requisitioned by the German Navy and stationed at Brest. On April 14, 1943, totally bereft of all anti-aircraft defenses she was attacked and sunk by RAF combat aircraft, South of St. Matthew point, after being completely burnt by two 550

A - A large number of fish, especially ballan wrasse (Labrus bergylta), inhabit the area between the two engines of the wreck of the buoy-layer.

B - Covered by jewel anemones (Corynactis viridis), the crane still dominates the bridge.

C - The sheet metal at the foot of the crane is totally covered by jewel anemones and alcyonarians.

D - A school of poor cod (Trisopterus minutus) hides between the engines.

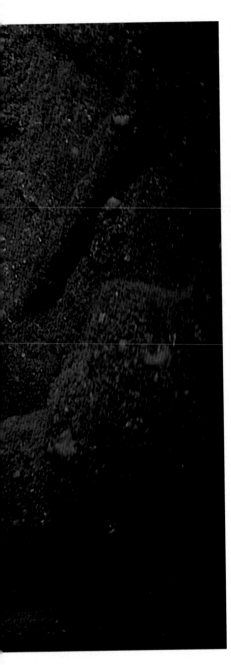

Kg. bombs. Today, her wreckage lies at a depth of 26 metres on a bed of coarse sand, interspersed by rocky masses at 1.6 miles and 187° from St. Matthew point. The coordinates for locating her using GPS are: 48°18′42″ North and 04°46′26″West.

Located a little off the narrow entrance that provides access to the Brest roadstead, the wreck is exposed to the wind and to the powerful sea swell. She is only protected from northern winds. Visits to this wreck must be undertaken only during fair weather, without wind. While the current is negligible or moderate at low levels of slack water, it can become strong or even violent at other times. During periods of fair weather, visibility often exceeds twenty metres. The vessel lies upright on the seabed, although it is broken into two unwedged parts that lie several metres

apart. To visit the *Emile Allard* in the best of conditions, divers should get into the water as close as possible to the stem. As soon as they enter the water, they should go down to the seabed so as to admire the spectacular stem while coming back up. The stem is quite a sight, standing upright in the water. The diving party should then proceed along the starboard side of the hull that features a gaping breach. The forecastle head still supports the huge windlass that was used to life the anchors of buoys. The bulwark is still intact for several metres. But the most impressive of the forward section of the vessel, is the crane, standing upright with its long horizontal beam. When the water is sufficiently clear, this beam can be seen in its entirety, offering a wonderful, unreal sight. The bow of the vessel gradually sinks into the sand, until it disappears entirely. The diving expedition continues with a visit to the after section of the vessel, damaged beyond recognition. Only the rounded part of the stern, bizarrely oriented at a right angle, is still visible in the midst of heap of piled and scattered metal. All this is an incredible jumble of metal in the midst of which two electric diesel

engine units are clearly visible. It is precisely at this point, at the engine room, that the vessel was hit by the bomb that sank her, killing three seamen. The visit ends by returning to the forward section of the vessel, to pass under the crane beam so as to reach the anchor line that, obviously, was secured as soon as the diving party reached the seabed. The wreck of the *Emile Allard* is home to large number of whiting-pouts, that in certain areas, are so densely packed, they seem like walls. Divers will also come across an equally large number of wrasses all over the wreck, and in some areas, conger-eels, will push their heads out from under a heap of twisted metal and narrow recesses without a trace of fear of the divers. Around the wreck, it is not uncommon to spot a large anglerfish perfectly camouflaged against the seabed. Despite the relatively moderate depth of the dive, a visit to the *Emile Allard* is not advisable for beginners, especially because of the strong currents around the wreck. All divers are well advised to contact one of the Brest-based diving centres that organise diving tours of the wreck on a regular basis.

E - The famous stem of the buoy-layer is planted vertically into the seabed at a depth of 27 metres. It is home to large number of invertebrates.

F - Cuckoo wrasses and other wrasses have made their home around the fore winch.

G - Under the crane, colonies of alcyonarians (Alcyonium digitatum) adorn the bridge.

H - A large number of conger eels hide amongst the pipes at the foot of the crane.

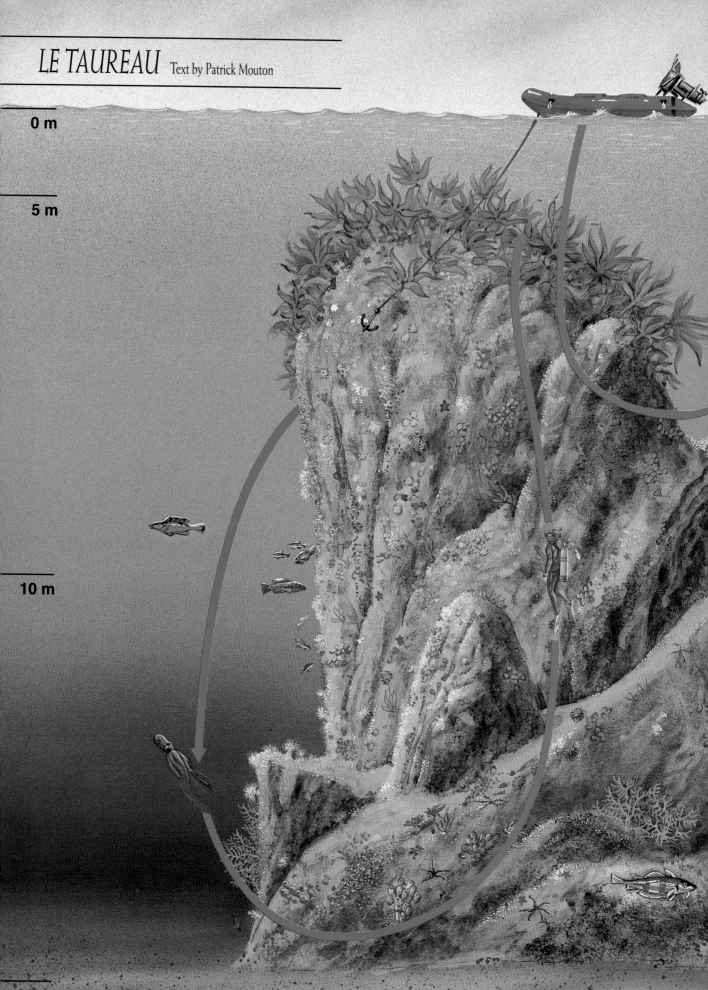

LE TAUREAU   Text by Patrick Mouton

0 m

5 m

10 m

22 m

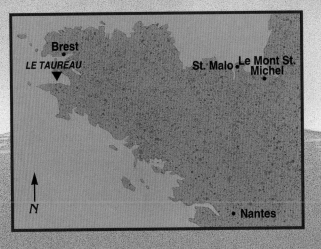

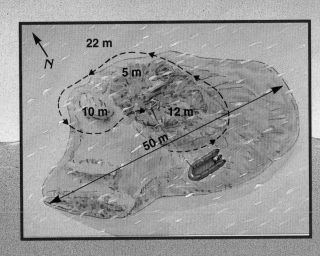

A - In spring, octopuses (Octopus vulgaris) frequent the bay of Douarnenez in hordes, congregating especially at the Taureau.

B - On the seabed, at a depth of 25 metres, a large number of invertebrates colonise the rocks: alcyonarians (Alcyonaium digitatum) and feather-star (Antedon bifidus) share the rocks with delicate ophiuroids (Ophiothrix fragilis).

C - Laminaria (Laminaria hyperborea) cover the summit of the rock.

To the South of the roadstead of Brest, the peninsula of Crozon in the Iroise sea, is one of the most beautiful diving locations in Brittany. The bay of Douamenez is particularly rich in interesting sites, with a large number of wrecks and scattered rocks. *Le Taureau*, located in the northern part of the bay is one of these rocks. Covered by brown seaweed, it culminates at two metres below the surface at low tide. With northern and eastern winds, when the water is clear, as is frequently the case, the rock can be seen from above the surface. With southern and western winds, on the other hand, the area is very exposed and soon becomes inaccessible. Currents are weak or negligible in this area. *Le Taureau* is located at 1.8 miles from the port of Crozon-Morgat and lies 350 metres North of another rock that can be seen from the surface even at high tide. This rock is known as 'Pierre Profonde' or Deep Stone. *Le Taureau* is therefore easily found, although to find it and dive in the area, the best solution is to use the services of one of the local diving centres such as the "Isa" centre (BP 5, Port de Plaisance, 29160, Crozon-Morgat).

C

D

D - It is not uncommon to encounter a monkfish (Lophius piscatorius) on the sandy seabed around the rock.

E - At the summit of the rock, spiny star fish (Marthasterias glacialis) invade the rocks and feed on mussels.

F - The northern face of the Taureau is scattered with large green or mauve-coloured common sea urchins (Eschinus esculentus).

G - Cuckoo wrasses (Labrus mixtus), a very coloured variety native to the Atlantic deep, can been seen only at depths greater than 20 metres.

A

B

E

Divers generally go into the water just above the rock, although one must be particularly careful if the vessel used features a high level of draught. About 30 metres in diameter, *Le Taureau* is made up of two rocky masses, separated by a large cleft. These rocky masses drop to depth of 21 metres to culminate in a debris of rocks lying on a seabed covered with coarse sand and Maêrl, the name given to a calcareous seaweed commonly found in Brittany. The northern face of the larger of the two rocks drops vertically to the seabed. Diving is generally undertaken by moving in between the two rocks as soon as one gets into the water, and then proceeding eastward so as to go around the larger rock, keeping the vertical face to one's left. A few arm-strokes brings the diver to the vertical face, richly covered with corynactis anemones, also known as pearl anemones, that appear in multicoloured patches to create a pretty carpet effect. The vertical face seems to become a real multicoloured mural fresco, interrupted with patches of orange-hued, rounded digitatum alcyonarians and red glomeratums. The entire rock face is also colonised by a large number of invertebrates, such as large, almond-green or mauve coloured sea urchins that are particularly photogenic, very voluminous feathery Metridium anemones etc. Upon reaching the sandy seabed, it is well worth one's while to observe the underwater life that inhabits it, especially the large number of black brittle stars and very beautiful and delicate seven-branched starfish of the Luidia ciliaris family. One can then

explore the western and southern rock faces that unfold towards the seabed in steps, interspersed with large patches of digitatum alcyonarians. This area is also home to a large number of white and brown striped whiting-pouts, caplins of a more golden hue, not to mention a variety of different coloured rockfish and wrasses. While re-surfacing, one must only go around the rock until one

reaches the cleft that separates the two rocky masses. At this point, the diving party may choose to re-surface or to explore the faces of the smaller rock. One of the main attractions of diving at Le Taureau is to be able to observe the 'coquettes', the local name for a kind of rockfish that is quite common in Brittany and immediately recognisable because of its splendid royal blue and orange-hued mantle. These creatures are not aggressive and because of their 'tropical' colours, are a real boon to underwater photographers. Lastly, during this dive that is not particularly difficult and that is well-protected from the winds coming in from the sea, with a little luck, one may come across a Peter's fish lazily swimming above a carpet of brown seaweed at the summit of the rock

F

G

THE WRECK OF THE PERLE

Text by Patrick Mouton

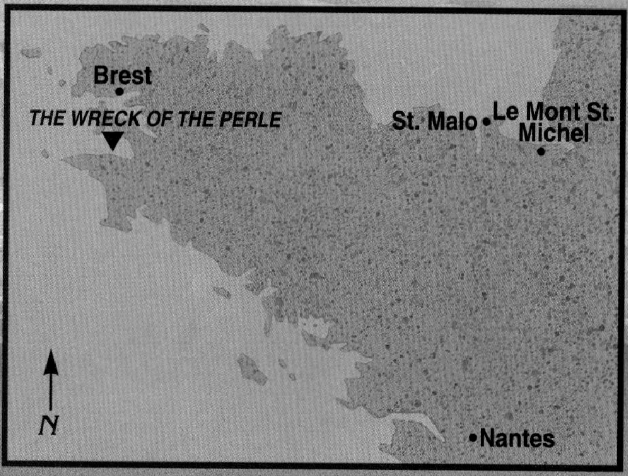

Brest
THE WRECK OF THE PERLE
St. Malo • Le Mont St. Michel
• Nantes
N

0 m

22 m

26 m

30 m

26 m

22 m

30 m

54 m

A - Plumose anemones (Metridium senile) have taken root all over the wreck, especially in front of the bridge.

B - A large number of alcyonarians (Alcyonium digitatum) have anchored on all the railings that surround the bridge.

C - The port side gangplank is draped with feather-star (Antedon bifida). Care must be taken to avoid fishing nets that are dangerous to divers.

D - As soon as the diver gets onto the upper deck of the Perle, he is greeted with an impressive wealth of invertebrates such as alcyonarians (Alcyonium digitatum) that carpet the hull and the large number of bib (Trisopterus luscus) that swim around in tight schools.

E - After she sank, the training trawler, the Perle, was raised, cleaned and submerged once again in the middle of the bay of Douarnenez.

Launched in 1971 at Dunkirk, this 54 metre long school trawler, proceeding at full speed, hit a rocky outcrop, 'Basse Jaune', located at the southern mouth of the bay of Douamenez. Although there was a breach in her hull several metres long, the vessel managed to continue towards her destination. She was then towed, but once she reached the port of Douamenez, she sank in shallow water. Declared a total write-off by experts, in March 1985, she was raised and then towed to the centre of the bay, in an area that already contained two other wrecks – the Meuse, a 70 metre long vessel and the Castel Meur, a 40 m. long trawler. Located close to each other, the three wrecks are now part of a reserve in which all fishing is totally prohibited.

The Perle lies on her keel, slightly leaning on her starboard side, on a sandy seabed, at a depth of 31 metres, 5 miles from Douamenez and Crozon-Morgat, right in the middle of the bay. To locate her using GPS, the geographical coordinates are: 48°09'18" North and 04°24'50" West. Since it is not very easy to find the wreck, divers should contact the Isa diving centre at Crozon-Morgat or the Douamenez Aquaclub, Villa Cornic, Plage des Sables Blancs, 29100 Douamenez. As far as the weather is concerned, The Perle is very exposed to south-westerly and westerly winds, that can raise a powerful swell.

The wreck is only accessible in stable, calm, fair weather with a slight northerly wind veering eastwards. It is only then that the water clears, affording underwater visibility of about 15 metres. Currents around the three wrecks are negligible or weak, reaching

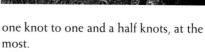

one knot to one and a half knots, at the most.

Given the size of the wreck, two dives are required to really visit The Perle in detail. In both cases, the divers should dive into the water as close as possible to the wreck, so as to be able to reach the ship's bridge immediately upon submerging.

The perfectly intact bridge lies at 22 metres below the surface. If possible, a diver ought to be sent to secure the anchor line to the top of the bridge. The first dive should be devoted to visiting the vessel's bow by going around the stempost on the port side, and then exploring the forward deck that lies two or three metres above the seabed. Divers should then return to the rear of the cabins to resurface between the two funnels. Second option: upon reaching the bridge, proceed along the starboard side

F - Schools of bib swim constantly over the deck, against a backdrop of plumose anemones (Metridium senile) that cover the hull.

G - On the Perle's capstans, totally covered by delicate ophiuroids (Ophiothrix fragilis).

E

F

G

towards the stern, so as to admire the propeller, still intact and in place. Then go return swimming above the large stern deck, up to the funnels before resurfacing ... not forgetting to remove the anchor line from the bridge.

While its white colour is still very visible today, over the years *The Perle* has taken on a covering of pastel-coloured alcyonarians and Metridium anemones with orange, green, white or brown tentacles. As a result, using a torch will reveal a colourful spectacle of underwater life, rarely found on wrecks off the French coast. It is quite clear that the ban on fishing has started bearing fruit. The darker nooks of the wreck have become home to a large number of sometimes oversized conger-eels and multitude of crustaceans, small crabs, lobsters and hermit-crabs.

Above the bridge and on the stern deck, thousands of whiting-pouts form compact clouds that dash around in the water. Wrasses, saithes and sea-basses are to be found aplenty all over the wreck, some weighing over five or six kilograms. In fact, *The Perle* is teeming with marine life and the only negative aspect at this diving site, is that it is only accessible to experienced divers because of its depth which is rather uncommon in Breton waters, and its location, far from the coast.

But what a feast for the eyes!!

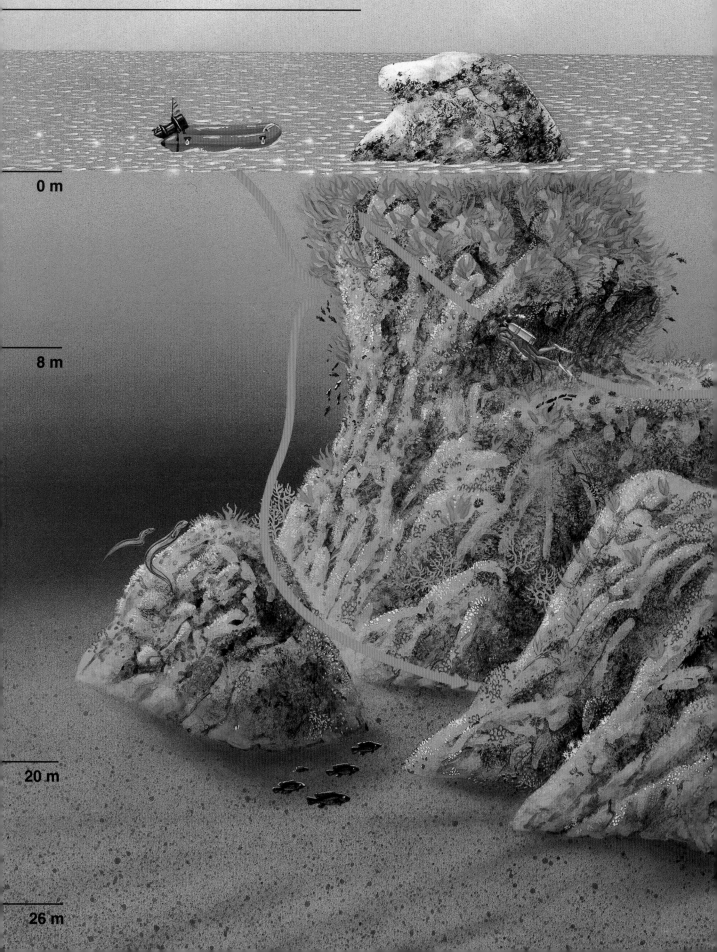

LE COCHON   Text by Patrick Mouton

0 m

8 m

20 m

26 m

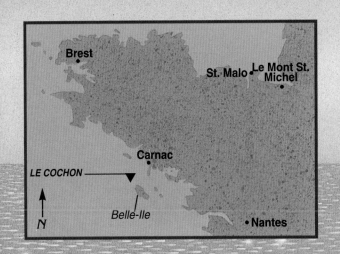

Brest

St. Malo • • Le Mont St.
                        Michel

Carnac

LE COCHON ➔ ▼

Belle-Ile

• Nantes

N

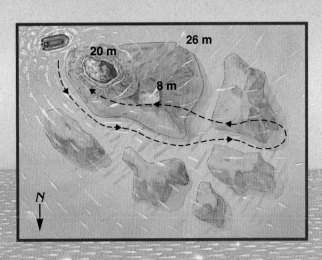

26 m

20 m

8 m

N

A

At 17 kilometres in length, Belle-Ile is the longest island in Brittany, featuring verdant dales that culminate in a rocky coastline, interspersed with superb beaches. The island boasts two picturesque fishing ports that are amongst the most beautiful on the French Atlantic coast. The rock Le Cochon (the Pig) lies 500 metres to the West of the north-westernmost tip of the island, Poulains point, so dear to the famous French actress Sarah Bernhardt. The rock, which rises slightly above the surface at low tide, lies on the shipping route that skirts the coast and is a navigational hazard. Le Cochon is not be confused with another rocky mass known as Les Chambres (the Rooms), located North of Poulains point. Le Cochon affords a splendid dive, at a site that is

B

only accessible in fair weather, since it is exposed to all winds, except the easterly winds, and that too, only if they are light to moderate. Furthermore, the current in this area is very strong and diving must only be undertaken at slack water, preferably at low tide. It must however be pointed out that currents can only be felt on the surface. Deeper underwater,

C

A - In the fissures of the rocks, one frequently comes across large conger eels (Conger conger).

B - Close to the surface, a field of laminaria hyperborea covers all the fixed underwater creatures anchored to the rocks.

resurface slowly, while exploring the other rock face, featuring a gentle slope. The entire area is interspersed with fissures that are home to a large number of filtering invertebrates such as sponges and other fixed marine creations, - gorgonias and alcyonarians – that feed on plankton particles carried in suspension by the current. As far as fish go, the site is a meeting point for a large number of wrasses, some of which weigh well over 2 kg, attracted here by the carpet of mussels that covers the rock, close to the surface. In spring, hundreds of crabs converge on and around the rock. During long spells of fair weather, the clarity of the water allows visibility from the surface up to a depth of fifteen metres, sometimes more. This diving site makes for a very enjoyable dive, without particular difficulties. However, the current and heavy marine traffic, especially in summer, combine to make good surface assistance services essential.

C - In the corridors that channel the current, gorgonians open up to feed.

D - A sample of a rock face completely covered by jewel anemones (Corynactis viridis).

E - Atlantic currents promote the development of the large laminaria hyperborea, yellow alcyonarian invertebrates (Alcyonium digitatum) as well as jewel anemones (Corynactis viridis).

F - Multi-coloured jewel anemones (Corynactis viridis) generally anchor away from light.

D

E

in the shadow of the rock, currents are nearly always moderate. Before casting anchor, one must take the precaution of placing the vessel well clear of the rock to avoid all risks of grounding. The anchor must also be cast downstream of the dominant current.

As is often the case with Breton diving sites around isolated rocks, diving at Le Cochon, doesn't go beyond a depth of about 20 metres. Upon getting into the water, divers should keep close to the eastern face of the rock that is totally covered by corynactics anemones – colonies of small 'pearl' anemones that come in all colours, in uniform patches – affording an absolutely breath-taking and uniquely 'Atlantic' spectacle. Once the divers reach the seabed at a depth of 20 metres, they only need to head north and

F
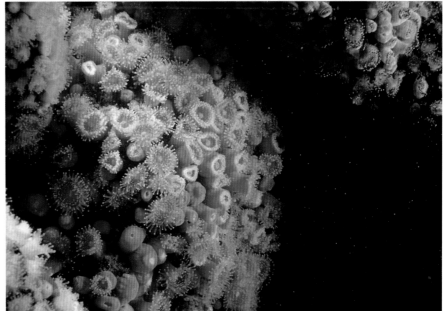

Fauna and flora of the Northern Sea

The northern seas, an ideal grouping that includes the part of the Atlantic that stretches from Gibraltar to the British and Irish coasts and continues eastwards to the North Sea, offer landscapes that are in sharp contrast to those encountered by divers in Mediterranean waters. Obviously, divers coming to the Mediterranean for the first time after experiencing northern waters, will also be similarly surprised. The reason for these contrasts, is the marine life to be found in these waters, although in many cases, the underwater species on both sides of Gibraltar, are the same.

The history and evolution of the Mediterranean has revealed that it was basically formed as an appendix to the Atlantic Ocean and that a large number of underwater organisms from the bordering ocean have adapted, over time, to the warmer Mediterranean waters. This is why it is not surprising to come across a conger eel off the British coast or a thornback ray in Brittany or even a sea anemone along the western coast of Scotland. Although colour and size may change (in favour of Atlantic specimen), most species will remain easily identifiable by all divers, regardless of their nationality.

The organisms that live in northern waters basically belong to two categories: the so-called Lusitanian species that inhabit the waters from Gibraltar up to the English Channel and the Atlantic-Boreal species that live in waters extending from the British isles up to the North Sea. A marine life of the Baltic Sea, that features peculiar hydrographic characteristics, falls into another category altogether. This is because the salinity of the Baltic varies from the typical salt water of the open sea to almost fresh water, resulting from the input of the large rivers that flow into it.

Temperature and visibility are the two aspects that are most likely to influence and characterise these waters. Paradoxically, temperatures may be higher towards the North and towards the South. The central and northern coasts of the British Isles are exposed to the Gulf Stream current that pushes warm Atlantic water up to Scotland, in currents so strong and some of this water ends up at the northernmost reaches of the North Sea that is home to a greater number of Atlantic species than that found in the more southern areas of the basin. As a matter of fact, the southern areas are not exposed to this current, as land masses prevent the Gulf Stream from bringing its favourable influx, isolating large masses of water that are therefore more sensitive to seasonal changes. The shallower mean depths of southern waters (50 m), also play their part in ensuring that these seas are more sensitive to seasonal changes. These differences are not very noticeable in summer but become more tangible in the cold months, when, for instance, the Irish and Cornwall coasts feature waters with surface temperatures of 9°C, as compared with values of 5-6°C in the North Sea. For divers using dry suits (advisable in these waters), the difference may not seem very much, but it is of prime importance to marine creatures and results in clear variations in underwater populations. Another feature of these seas is transparency. With rare exceptions, the water in northern seas is generally veiled, with dominant green and bluish hues, reducing visibility to way below mean Mediterranean levels. Naturally, these are merely general indications, since, in practice, a great deal depends on individual diving sites. Visibility will tend to be more favourable in areas directly exposed to Atlantic currents and will tend to fall in sheltered areas, estuarial waters or seabeds affected by bottom flowing currents. Underlying all this however, is the intrinsic wealth of the Atlantic waters that, thanks to an abundance of nutrients, support the prolific development of plancton that

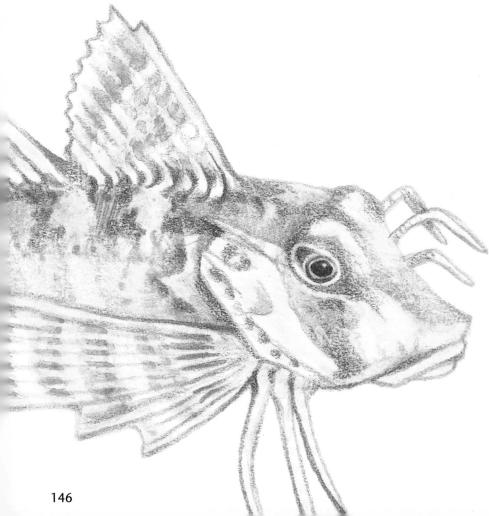

supplies a rich food chain. The abundance of life-giving plancton is one of the reasons that Atlantic specimens tend on an average to be larger than their southern cousins. Divers are well advised to bear in mind that plancton proliferation peaks between April and May, drastically reducing underwater visibility. The plancton and nutrient content of the water gradually falls, however, and general diving conditions (including temperature) improve in summer, before briefly returning to spring conditions in the fall, when the marine life that was nurtured earlier in the year is still very visible, as it awaits the changes that come with winter. Another important difference between northern and Mediterranean waters, that has considerable impact on diving, from both a biological and practical viewpoint, is the issue of tides. While differences between high and low tides generally range between 3 and 7 metres in these waters, differences of 10 m are not rare. This means that diving times must be carefully planned, since underwater conditions, especially strong tidal currents that can try the swimming skills of the most experienced diver, can change drastically when the tide turns. However, the vast areas of seabed left uncovered by the tide provide a unique occasion to enjoy a sort of dry diving experience that will prove amply satisfying to any diver in love with natural history. At any rate, although diving in northern seas undeniably entails certain difficulties that can easily be overcome, these waters are rich in marine life, thanks, in no small measure, to their variable coastline. A quick straight overview of the coastal profile reveals that the straits and protected rias of Spain cede to the rocky seabed at Biarritz, featuring high calcareous cliffs that in turn, as one proceeds northward, make way for the dunes and sandy plains created by the delta of the Gironde, and still further north, for the calcareous coasts of Normandy. The coast of Brittany is, on the other hand, a labyrinth of small islands, beaches and straits, that provide for interesting underwater landscapes that are completely different from the rocky coasts sculpted into the shores of Calvados by the same sea that crashes against the white cliffs of Le Havre and Boulogne, ideally linked by a sandy bed to the cliffs of Dover. Although these cliffs are hard, they are easily erodable by marine animals that make their dens in the large number of cracks and fissures in the rockface. This natural habitat is lacking along the more sandy shores of Great Britain and along the volcanic cliffs that make up the coast of Scotland.

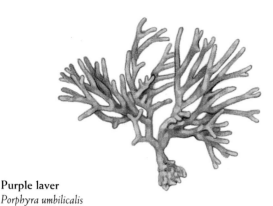

Purple laver
Porphyra umbilicalis

Red seaweed with a gelatinous thallus that is laminar in appearance. Irregularly lobed, it anchors to the substrate using branched filaments. It is purple red in colour. It grows both in protected areas and areas exposed to currents, on rocky seabeds in the midtidal to splash zone. It can attain 60 cm in length. This is an edible seaweed and is eaten both raw and cooked.

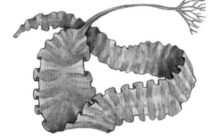

Kelp
Laminaria digitata

Large brown seaweed with a thallus made up of frond divided into blades that are almost always arranged in a fan, all attached to a very flexible stem anchored to the substrate by a series of branched root-like stems. It is brownish in colour and grows on rocky bottoms in the intertidal area. It is easily visible at low tide and can grow to a height of 3 to 4 metres. This seaweed is commercially important since it is a valuable source of alginates.

Japweed
Sargassum muticum

Brown alga with a clearly branched central stem. Each branch has elongated, indented leaves that bear at their base, a floating bladder a few millimeters across. This seaweed is yellow–brown in colour. It grows in sheltered areas on hard seabeds, between the low tide mark and a depth of 20 metres. It can grow to several metres in length. This seaweed that is now widespread along Atlantic coasts, originates from Japan and reached European coasts in the 1960s, mixed with oysters imported from the Pacific.

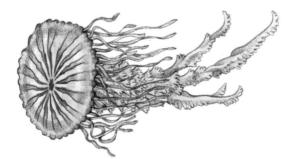

ALGAE
Spongy weed
Codium tomentosum

Green seaweed with a spongy and clearly branched thallus. The branches are cylindrical and covered with very fine filaments. Bright green in colour, this species grows on hard substrates up to a depth of 20 metres from the surface. It can grow up to 30 cm in height.

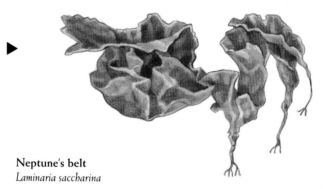

Neptune's belt
Laminaria saccharina

Large brown alga with a thallus made up of a laminar, undulated fronds that are anchored by a small holdfast at the end of a short tough stem. It is greenish brown in colour. It grows in sheltered areas on rocky seabeds, at depths varying from mid-tide to 20 m. It can grow to a height of three metres. Its Latin name is due to the formation of sugar crystals on its surface when dried.

Fucus vesicolosus

A brown bush-like alga made up of short fronds featuring a central vein and dichotomic branching (i.e. they divide into two halves). The blades are provided with floating bladders. This alga is more or less dark olive green in colour. It grows on rocky seabeds in the tidal area where it forms a rather thick covering. It can grow to 70 cm in length.

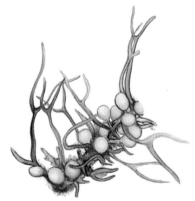

INVERTEBRATES

Compass jellyfish
Chrysaora hysoscella

Jellyfish with a smooth and slightly convex umbrella and an edge featuring 32 lines separated by dark radial bands and 24 tentacles grouped in threes. Four oral arms that span a length of 5-6 times its diameter leave from its mouth. It comes in a variety of colours but the randial bands are always yellow–brown. It bears a spot at the top of the umbrella. It is frequently found inshore, especially in summer. It can grow to 30 cm in diameter.

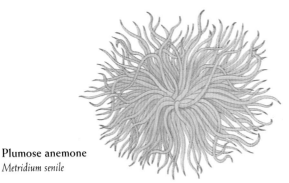

Plumose anemone
Metridium senile

Sea anemone of varying appearance with wide and irregular base and very high column that reveals a pre-eminent margin when completely extended. The length and number of the tentacles vary (up to 200). In individuals with shorter and more numerous tentacles, the anemone takes on a feathery appearance. Colouring varies from white to orange. This anemone anchors onto hard substrates, favouring darker areas, at depths varying from just a few metres to 100 metres. It can attain a height of 30 – 50 centimetres.

Jewel anemone
Corynactis viridis

Short sea anemone with a diameter that is less than the base disc. The short tentacles, featuring a spheric point, are arranged in radial rows in increasing order of length. This species anchors in great numbers to hard surfaces in dark areas, starting at a depth of at least five metres. Colouring is very variable (from green to purple) and, as a general rule, the tips of the tentacles are lighter. It can measure up to 2.5 cm in diameter.

Lobster
Homarus gammarus

Large crustacean featuring very strong and assymetrical claws and a smooth carapace. Close to the eyes, at the sides of the pointed rostellum, there are two pairs of antennae: the first are forked and short while the second are very long. Shell colouring is bluish-black with yellow marbling on the back. It lives on sandy seabeds to a depth of about 60 metres. It can grow to a length of 50 cm.

Anemonia sulcata

Anthozoan distinguished by a large leg that is firmly anchored to the substrate and a rather short column that holds up to 200 thin, mobile tentacles that area only partially retractable. The surface is covered with sticky, stinging cells that block and kill prey (small fish, crustaceans, organic detritus). Colouration varies from greenish to brown to greyish. The tentacles generally have purplish tips and contain zooxantelle. It lives in shallow pools well exposed to light, at depths of up tp 20 m. It grows to 20 –25 cm in diameter.

Dahlia anemone
Tealia felina

Sea anemone with highly adherent suction cup and a column with its lower part covered with tubercles that capture a large quantity of detritus that partly camouflages its body. Its tentacles, that vary between 80 and 160 in number, are short, stock and retractible. The column is generally light coloured while the disc is red-striped. The tentacles often feature light and dark bands. It generally lives in pools or dark fissures between the surface and a depth of 100 m.

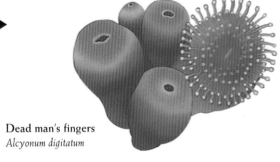

Dead man's fingers
Alcyonum digitatum

This alcyonnarian develops in massive fleshy colonies. It is distinguished by its finger-shaped branches. Its translucent polyps are dispersed irregularly on the surface of the colonies and can be retracted or expanded. Each polyp has finely branched tentacles. Colouring is generally white or orange, although yellowish or brownish specimens have been found. It grows on hard substrates, at depths varying from justa few metres to 50 metres below the surface. It can grow to a height of 20 cm.

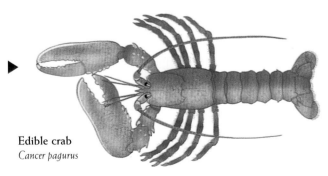

Edible crab
Cancer pagurus

Crab with a large oval shell, featuring an indented front and side border. The forehead is narrow and not prominent. The claws are quite similar to each other, with large indentations. Colouring is reddish brown with black claw tips. It lives in subtidal waters, up to depths of about 100 metres. It feeds on fish, crustaceans, molluscs and echinoderms. It can grow to about 25 cm in width.

Spider crab
Maja squinado

Carb with an oval-shaped shell that is very convex both longitudinally and transversally. The shell is covered by knobs and spines in which seaweed and detritus often gets caught, providing the crab with camouflage. The rostellum is made up of two straight spines. The claw bearing arms or chelae are more or less of the same size as the other arms. Shell colouring is brownish or yellowish red. This crab lives close to rocky bottoms at depths varying from just a few metres to 50 metres. It can attain up to 20 cm in width.

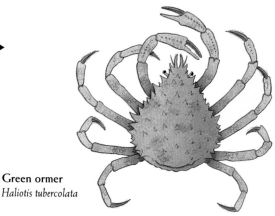

Green ormer
Haliotis tubercolata

Mollusc with flat ear-shaped shell that bears a series of holes allowing the creature to breathe. Short syphons linked to these holes allow the ormer to exhale. The outer surface is rough with radial ribbings that correspond to the creature's periods of growth. Inside the shell is smooth nacre. The large fleshy leg is greenish and surrounded by frilly tentacles. It lives on rocky bottoms between the surface and a depth of 1015 m.

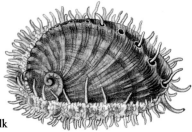

Common whelk
Buccinum undatum

Spindle-shaped mollusc that is rather thick and features axial and spiral ribbing. The last spiral turn is wide and makes up 70% of the entire shell. The aperture is large and oval-shaped with a thin outer lip that goes through a wide arc before joining the short syphon canal. This mollusc has a large, tough food and tentacles on its head, The eyes are located at the base of the tentacles, together with a long proboscis. Colouring is yellowish white with darker bands along the edges. It lives on hard and mobile bottoms, at depths varying from just a few metres up to 1,000 m below the surface. It can attain a length of 10-12 cm.

Grey sea slug
Aeolidia papillosa

Nudibranch with a rather wide, flat body that become pointed at the rear. The back features a large number of long cerata, with a bald patch at the centre. Oral tentacles and rhinophores are well developed. Colouration varies from cream to brown, and from orange pink to dark purple. The cerata are always white-tipped. This species preys voraciously on anemones and other actinal creatures. It lives in shallow coastal waters on rocky seabeds. It can grow to 12 cm in length.

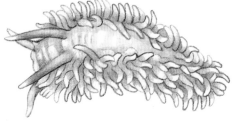

Sea lemon
Archidoris pseudoargus

Elongated, oval-shaped leathery nudibranch. The mantle bears many short rounded tubercles of varying size, while the short cone-shaped rhinophores are located on the head. This species has multiple, three-fined gills. Colouring is light brown with varied coloured mottling (green, yellow, red). This species lives between the surface and a depth of 300 metres on rocky bottoms where the sponge on which it feeds, Halichondria panicea, is especially abundant. It can attain a length of 12 cm.

Soft shell clam
Mya arenaria

Large bivalve mollusc with more or less oval shape. The right valve is more convex than the left. The surface of the shell is decorated by fine concentric growth markings. The inside of the shell clearly bears the pri of the muscles that are used to close the valves. The mollusc has a very developed foot and two very long syphons that rise above the sediment which the animal buries itself. It lives on sandy and sandy-muddy bottoms, at depths varying from just a few metres to about 20 m. It can grow to up to 15 cm.

Scallop
Pecten maximus

Bivalve mollusc with an unmistakable shape since the left valve is flat and the right valve markedly convex. Both bear large radial ribbings. Several tentacles can be seen coming out of the half-closed valves. These serve as feelers and chemoreceptors. Juveniles are anchored to the substrate, although adults can move freely in the water by forcefully flapping their valves. This species lies on its right valve on sandy and shingle bottoms, up to 100 m below the surface. It can attain a diameter of 15 cm.

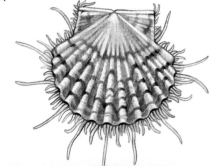

Common octopus
Octopus vulgaris

Cephalopod mollusc with a globulous head that is very distinct from the rest of its body that is made up of eight tentacles featuring a double row of suction cups. The laterally positioned, perfectly functioning eyes are clearly visible on the head. On its belly, this species has a narrow aperture from which a short siphon tube extends. Colouring is very varied, given the considerable camouflage capabilities of this species. It lives on rocky bottoms from the intertidal region up to 100 metres below the surface. When its tentacles are extended, it can stretch to a width of over one metre.

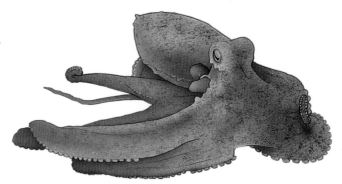

Brittle star
Ophiotrix fragilis

Ophiurod with a disc-shaped body featuring large radial scutes. Five slender arms covered by small radially arranged spines extend from these scutes. In many cases, the arms are deformed because of fractures. Colouring varies from bright red to purple and violet. It lives on various types of seabed, under rocks or amongst seaweed, from the intertidal area to depths of up to 300 metres.
It can attain a diameter of 10 cm.

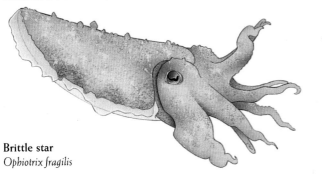

Common sun starfish
Crossaster papposus

Starfish with a typical rayed form and large disc surrounded by 8-16 stocky subtriangular arms featuring spines on their edges. The dorsal surface is entirely covered by small spines. Colouring is brownish red with whitish spots on the back, while the underside is yellowish white. It lives on rocky and sandy seabeds, at depths varying from about 10 metres to over 500 m. It can attain a diameter of 30-35 cm.

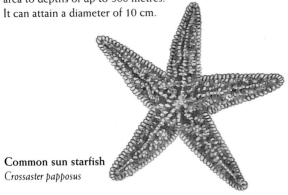

Sea cucumber
Holothuria forskali

Flat elongated body that is flat on the belly that features a large number of pedicles placed in three or four rows. The back is covered with cone-shaped papillae. The mouth is surrounded by about two short tentacles. Colouring is blackish brown with white papillae. This species lives on sandy bottoms rich in vegetation, at depths varying from the intertidal area to about 100 metres. It can grow to a length of 20 cm. If disturbed, it emits long, very sticky whitish filaments that discourages intruders.

Common cuttlefish
Sepia officinalis

Cephalopod mollusc with an flat, wide and elongated body featuring edges bordered by a narrow blade fin that it uses to move in the water. Four pairs of relatively short arms and two tentacles extend from the head. The tentacles are elastic and extendable, with suction cups only at the tips. Inside its body, the cuttlefish has its famous cuttlefish bone that provides the animal with its shape and also helps it maintain its balance in the water. Colouring is varied, because of its considerable camouflaging capabilities. It lives on a variety of seabeds, at depths varying from just a few metres to 200 m. It can grow up to 40 cm in length.

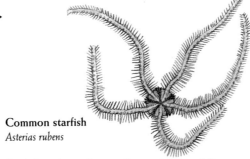

Common starfish
Asterias rubens

Starfish with a rather small central disc and five arms that are rounded at the base and pointed at the tip. The body is characterised by a rough surface, caused by irregularly arranged spines that are surrounded by special organs known as pedicellariae. Colouring ranges from red to yellowish brown. This species lives on hard seabeds, at depths varying from just a few metres to over 600 metres, often in large groups that favour locations close to banks of the molluscs on which it feeds. It can grow to a diameter of 50 cm.

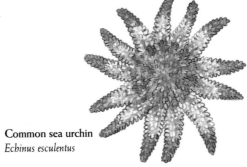

Common sea urchin
Echinus esculentus

Sea urchin with a globe-shaped body featuring short, dispersed spines. Shell colouring varies from red to purple with greenish hues, while the spines are reddish with violet tips. It lives, at depths varying betweem 10 and 40 metres, on sandy bottoms rich in laminaria on which it feeds. It can grow to 16 cm in diameter.

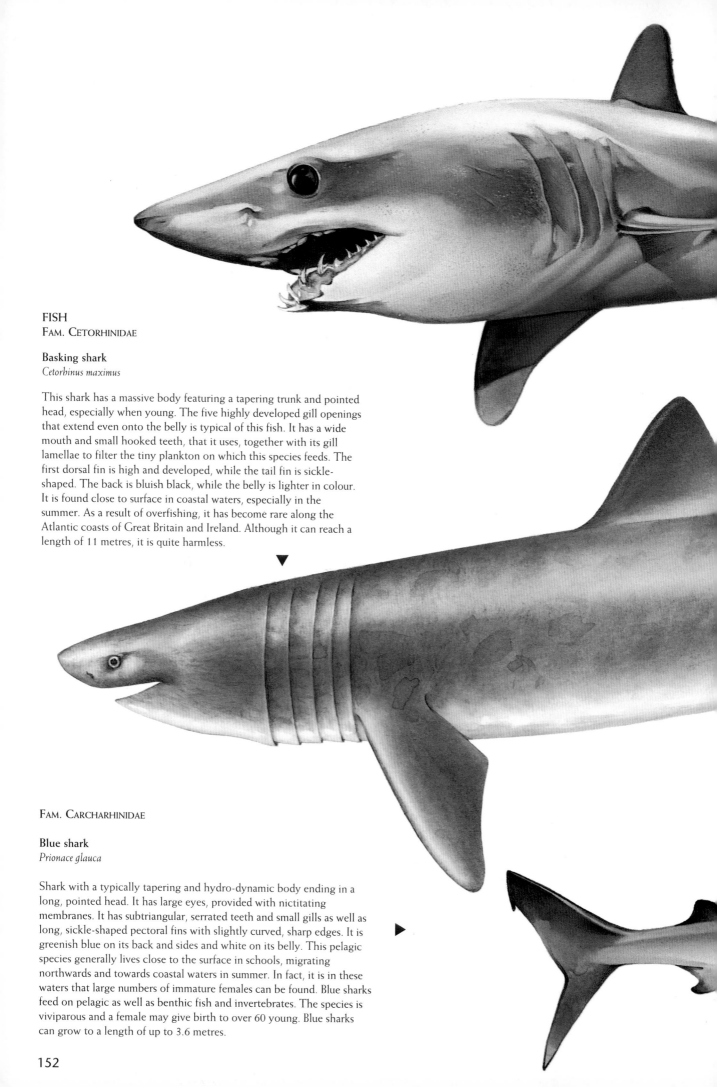

FISH
FAM. CETORHINIDAE

Basking shark
Cetorhinus maximus

This shark has a massive body featuring a tapering trunk and pointed head, especially when young. The five highly developed gill openings that extend even onto the belly is typical of this fish. It has a wide mouth and small hooked teeth, that it uses, together with its gill lamellae to filter the tiny plankton on which this species feeds. The first dorsal fin is high and developed, while the tail fin is sickle-shaped. The back is bluish black, while the belly is lighter in colour. It is found close to surface in coastal waters, especially in the summer. As a result of overfishing, it has become rare along the Atlantic coasts of Great Britain and Ireland. Although it can reach a length of 11 metres, it is quite harmless.

FAM. CARCHARHINIDAE

Blue shark
Prionace glauca

Shark with a typically tapering and hydro-dynamic body ending in a long, pointed head. It has large eyes, provided with nictitating membranes. It has subtriangular, serrated teeth and small gills as well as long, sickle-shaped pectoral fins with slightly curved, sharp edges. It is greenish blue on its back and sides and white on its belly. This pelagic species generally lives close to the surface in schools, migrating northwards and towards coastal waters in summer. In fact, it is in these waters that large numbers of immature females can be found. Blue sharks feed on pelagic as well as benthic fish and invertebrates. The species is viviparous and a female may give birth to over 60 young. Blue sharks can grow to a length of up to 3.6 metres.

FAM. LAMNIDAE

Short fin mako shark
Isurus oxyrhyncus

Large shark with a hydro-dynamic body and long pointed head. It has a wide mouth with long pointed teeth without cusps on both jaws. It has well developed gills located in front of the pectoral fins. The tail fin is crescent-shaped, with side carinae. The back of this fish is greyish blue, with a lighter colouring on the sides and a whitish belly. It lives close to the surface where it feeds mainly on small fish swimming in schools. The powerful and quick swimming movements of this fish allow it to spring several metres above the surface. An ovoviviparous species, this fish can grow up to 4 metres in length. It is considered dangerous to humans.

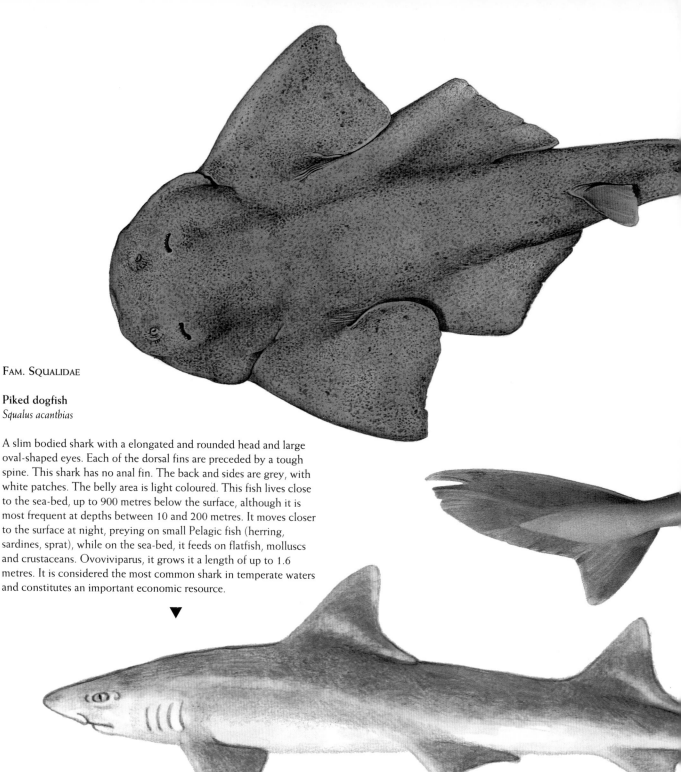

FAM. SQUALIDAE

Piked dogfish
Squalus acanthias

A slim bodied shark with a elongated and rounded head and large oval-shaped eyes. Each of the dorsal fins are preceded by a tough spine. This shark has no anal fin. The back and sides are grey, with white patches. The belly area is light coloured. This fish lives close to the sea-bed, up to 900 metres below the surface, although it is most frequent at depths between 10 and 200 metres. It moves closer to the surface at night, preying on small Pelagic fish (herring, sardines, sprat), while on the sea-bed, it feeds on flatfish, molluscs and crustaceans. Ovoviviparus, it grows it a length of up to 1.6 metres. It is considered the most common shark in temperate waters and constitutes an important economic resource.

▼

FAM. SCYLIORHINIDAE

Greater spotted dogfish
Scyliorhinus stellaris

Small shark with a fairly slim body and large flattened head. It has a very arched mouth that is always visible since it is not covered by nasal valves. The first dorsal fin is located immediately behind the pelvic fins that are quadrangular and partially separated in males. This fish is brownish grey on its back with large rounded dark patches on its side; its belly is whitish. This shark tends to live close to the sea-bed, especially detrital and rocky sea-beds, at depths that vary from just a few metres to over 100 metres. It can reach a length of 1.5 metres. It is rarer than the Scyliorhinus canicula (lesser spotted dogfish), of the same genus. ▶

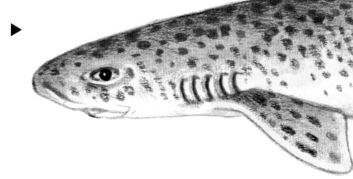

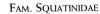

Monkfish
Squatina squatina

◀ Shark with a compressed body that thins greatly towards the tail.
This fish has a very large head. Its wide shape, similar to that of a
ray, is mainly due to its large pectoral and pelvic fins. It has a wide,
protrusible mouth and small, uniform teeth. It is greyish or grey
brown in colour with small patches that are dark on its back and
white on its belly. As its shape suggests, it is a bottom dwelling
shark, typically found on sandy or muddy sea-beds up to a depth of
150 metres, where it generally lies half buried to ambush its prey
that is mostly made up of flatfish, crustaceans and molluscs. It is
ovoviviparous and can reach a length of 1.8 metres.

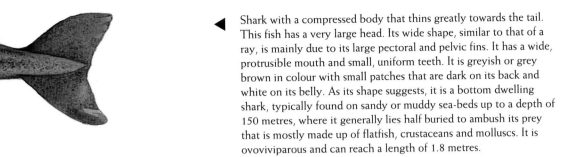

▲

FAM. TRIAKIDAE

Common smooth hound
Mustelus mustelus

Shark with a fairly tapering body and breathing hole. It has a fold of
skin running along its back, from the tail up to the gills. Its skin is
almost completely smooth. It is grey on its back and sides and white
on its belly. It preys mostly on crustaceans. This mainly nocturnal
fish tends to live close to the sea-bed in coastal waters with a sandy-
muddy bottom, from depths ranging from just a few metres up to
about 100 metres. Placentally viviparous, this species can reach a
length of up to 1.6 metres.

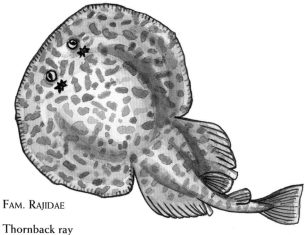

FAM. RAJIDAE

Thornback ray
Raja clavata

This fish has a flat, sub-rhomboidal body, with slightly sinuous edges towards the front. The tips of its pectoral fins are very acute. It has a large number of spines close to its eyes and along the nape of its neck. It has median and side spines on its tail. Side spines are typical of females that also have spiny scales on their bellies. This fish is grey or brownish grey with darker or yellowish patches. It lives on various kinds of sea-bed: sandy, muddy or detrital, mainly at depths of between 10 and 60 metres, especially during the summer months, although it can live at depths of several hundred metres. It preys on crustaceans and small fish (sandeels, flatfish, small codfish and herring). This oviparous species can grow to a length of up to 85 cm.

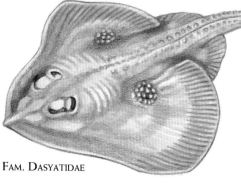

FAM. DASYATIDAE

Sting ray
Dasyatis pastinaca

This flat-bodied fish is shaped like a quadrangular disc that is slightly wider than it is long. The outer edges of the disc are rounded and the front edges are rather straight. Its long, thin tail features a dorsal carina and a marked abdominal fold. Although it has no tailfins, it has a strong sting at about the mid-point of the tail. Its back is generally smooth although adults frequently have bony knobs and blunt spines on their backs. This fish is generally olive-coloured on its back. Its belly is white, with blackish grey edges. Although its shape is perfectly adapted to the benthic life-style of rayfish, sting rays are often encountered in mid-water. It lives close to sandy and muddy sea-beds up to depths of about a hundred metres. It preys on molluscs and crustaceans, since its flat teeth serve as a grinder to break through their shells. Aplacentally viviparous, sting rays can reach a length of up to 2 metres.

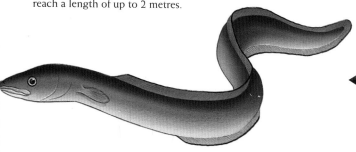

FAM TORPEDINIDAE

Marbled electric ray
Torpedo marmorata

This species has a disk-like body that is longer than it is wide, and ends in a short strong tail with a wide tail fin. The two dorsal fins are very close to each other, almost overlapping. Its small breathing holes behind the fish's eyes, are provided with 6-8 clearly distinguished fringes. Electric rays have a uniform or marbled brown back and a white belly. A benthic species, these rays live on sandy sea-beds at depths of up to 30 metres. They prey mainly on other benthic species that they stun with electric shocks. This ovoviviparous species can grow to up to 60 cm in length. It is more commonly encountered in summer and in the autumn.

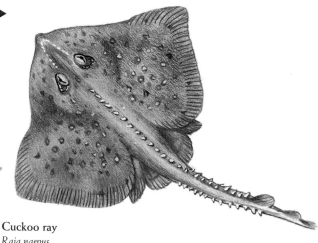

Cuckoo ray
Raja naevus

The front edges of this flat-bodied species are very curved and the tips of its pectoral fins are rounded. It has small spines on its back that tend to decrease at the centre of its finds. Series of small spines can also be found on the sides of its tail. It's grey brown or yellowish in colour with two eye-shaped yellow patches at the centre of the pectoral fins. The belly is white with dark, irregular patches. It lives on sandy and muddy sea-beds at depths ranging from 20 to 150 metres. It feeds on benthic invertebrates and fish. It is oviparous and can reach a length of 70 cm.

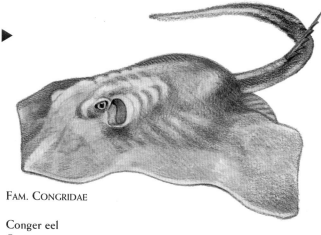

FAM. CONGRIDAE

Conger eel
Conger conger

An elongated, cylindrical body that ends in a long rounded head. The mouth is wide, with large lips and a prominent upper jaw. The dorsal fin starts at the pectoral fins, making this fish easily distinguishable from moray eels. Colour varies from black to light grey, depending on the habitat of the animal. Conger eels frequently inhabit deepwater wrecks. They feed on lesser fish, crab and squid. Conger eels spawn in the summer months. They grow to lengths of up to 2.8 metres.

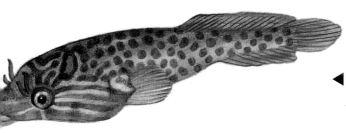

FAM. LOPHIIDAE

Angler fish
Lophius piscatorius

Flat-bodied fish with a very large head and front body that tapers to become slim towards the rear that ends in a large tail fin. The mouth is large and turned upwards, since the lower jaw is considerably larger than the upper. Angler fish have small, very mobile eyes, located on the top of their heads. The body is devoid of scales but features numerous small flaps of skin that increase the camouflage of this species. In front of the dorsal fin, there is a series of isolated rays, the foremost of which is particularly long and has a fleshy tip that the fish uses as a lure to entice its prey. Colouring on the back varies from reddish brown to greenish brown, while the belly is white. Angler fish tend to live on sandy or muddy sea-beds, but are also found close to rocks and algae, at depths varying between 10 and over 500 metres. This fish can grow to up to 2 metres in length.

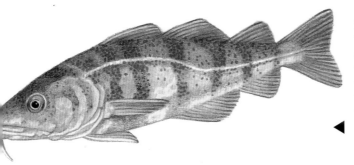

Pollack
Pollachius pollachius

A strong, but tapering body with three dorsal and two anal fins. The tail fin is concave. The lower jaw projects beyond the upper and there is no barbel on the chin. Body colouring is brown-olive or brown green on the back, with lighter sides and white belly. Pollack favour rocky sea-beds or large rock masses, located between the surface and a depth of 200 metres. In coastal or shallow waters (for instance, in estuarian waters), young 1-2 year old pollacks are more frequent, although it is not uncommon to come across adults. Pollack feed mainly on lesser fish. This species can attain a length of up to 1.3 metres.

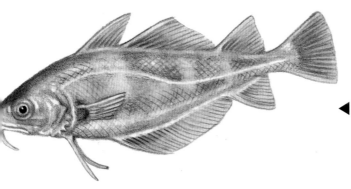

FAM. GOBIESOCIDAE

Shore clingfish
Lepadogaster lepadogaster

Small fish with a convex back and straight underside. The head is long and spatula-shaped, rounded at the mouth, with a prominent upper jaw. In front of its eyes, this fish has two tentacles, one of which is fairly long. The dorsal and anal fins are linked to the tail fin by a wide membrane. The suction anchoring organ that is typical of this family, is found on the belly of the fish. More or less light red in colour, shore clingfish have two large eye-shaped patches with blue centres. Shore clingfish live in shallow waters, anchoring to the lower part of rocks, using their suction organs. They feed on small invertebrates. They can reach a length of up to 6.5 cm.

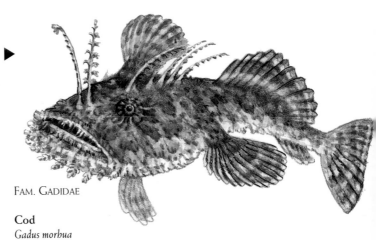

FAM. GADIDAE

Cod
Gadus morhua

Strong body with a long head and the upper jaw extending over the lower jaw, that features a well-developed chin barbel. Cod have three dorsal fins and a double anal fin. The tail is relatively short and truncated. Colouring on the back varies from greenish to brownish with more or less extensive mottling towards the sides. The belly is white. The species is found in a variety of habitats, from coastal waters to the open sea, at various depths, extending up to 600 metres. Schools of young cod are more frequent in shallow waters. The species feeds on lesser fish, crustaceans, words and other benthic invertebrates. Cod migrate over long distances to reach their breeding grounds. They can grow to lengths of over 1.2 metres.

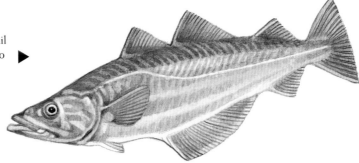

Pouting
Trisopterus luscus

A strong, particularly deep-bodied fish with three dorsal and two anal fins, all of which are contiguous. The rear margin of the tail fin is either straight or slightly concave. The upper jaw projects above the lower jaw that features a well-developed chin barbel. Body colouration in copper brown on the back with 4 to 5 dark vertical bands that extend towards the sides. The belly is white. There is a black spot at the base of the pectoral fins. Pouting are a schooling species and live in inshore waters at depths varying from 3 to 300 metres, close to rock faces and wrecks. Diet consists mainly of crustaceans and molluscs. They can attain a length of 40 cm.

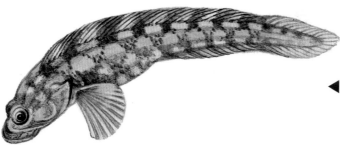

FAM. BELONIDAE

Garfish
Belone belone

A fish with a characteristically elongated, compressed body with a depressed tail stump. The head ends in two long jaws that form the typical needle beak. Body colouration is bright greenish blue on the back while the lower part of the flanks and belly are silver coloured. The species lives in small schools in surface waters, coming inshore during the spring and summer months. It feeds on small fish, small squid and pelagic crustaceans. It can attain a length of about 1 metre.

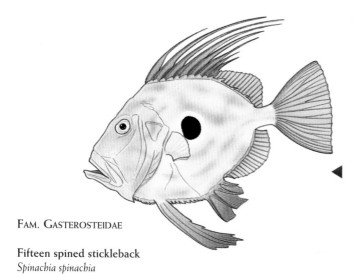

FAM. GASTEROSTEIDAE

Fifteen spined stickleback
Spinachia spinachia

Small fish with an elongated body that ends in a subtle tail stump. The head is pointed. Typical of this species are the approximately fifteen small spines, located in front of the dorsal fin. Body colouration is brownish or greenish on the back and yellowish on the belly. During the spawning season, however, males take on blue hues. This species lives inshore, close to sea-beds rich in vegetation, at depths of up to 10 metres below the surface. This fish feeds mainly on small crustaceans. It can grow up to 20 cm in length.

FAM. ZOARCIDAE

Eelpout
Zoarces viviparus

Elongated body that tapers towards the tail. The head is large and the mouth features thick lips. The dorsal fin and anal fin join at the tail fin. The pelvic fins are located just behind the throat. The skin is mucus covered. Body colouration varies from greyish brown to yellowish green depending on the habitat of the fish. The pectoral fins have yellow or orange margins. This species lives on sea-bed rich in seaweed, between the tidal depth and 40 metres below the surface. It feeds on crustaceans, molluscs and small fish. This is a viviparous species, that is to say, featuring uterine fertilisation and placental development of the foetus. It can attain a length of 50 cm.

FAM. ZEIDAE

John Dory
Zeus faber

Fish with a high, oval and very compressed body. The foremost part is characterised by spines and an oblique and straight profile from the head to the dorsal fin. This fish has large eyes placed high. Its mouth is very protrusible. The dorsal fin is well developed and features long filaments. A double row of spines runs along the belly. Body colouration is golden or silvery with longitudinal yellowish lines that are more visible on the lower part of the flanks. The dark round spot is typical of this species. This fish lives at sandy and muddy sea-beds, at depths varying between 10 and 200 m. It feeds on smaller fish, molluscs and crustaceans. It can attain a length of 60 cm.

FAM. SYNGNATHIDAE

Long-snouted sea horse
Hippocampus ramulosus

Underwater species with an unmistakable form featuring a body made up of a series of bony rings that end at one extremity in a fine, prehensile tail and at the other, in a characteristic horse's head with a long tubular snout. The head and the back are provided with fine skin appendages that are more developed in males. Body colouration is greyish brown with small white spots. This species inhabits coastal waters, close to sea-beds rich in seaweed or eelgrass, between the surface and a depth of 30 metres. It feeds on small crustaceans that are snapped up by the sucking action of the snout. Long-snouted sea horses can attain a length of 15 cm.

Greater pipefish
Syngnathus acus

Slim-bodied fish, rendered rather rigid by its series of rigid polygonal rings. The tail is not prehensile. The head is elongated and slim. This fish features a dorsal and anal fin as well as pectoral fins. It inhabits coastal waters, close to sandy and muddy bottoms. It feeds on small plankton. In the summer months, the males can be seen carrying the eggs that are about to hatch. This fish can attain a length of 45 cm.

FAM. SCORPAENIDAE

Red scorpionfish
Scorpaena scrofa

Strong-bodied fish with a convex dorsal profile and large head featuring spines and various growths that are more developed on the chin. The dorsal fin has tough spines linked to venomous glands that can cause painful stings. Body colouration is reddish with darker and lighter patches as well as yellow and orange coloured hues. This species lives close to rocky and detrital sea-beds, at depths varying between 20 and over 200 metres. It feeds on crustaceans that it ambushes lurking on the sea-bed, taking advantage of its natural camouflage. It can attain a length of up to 50 cm.

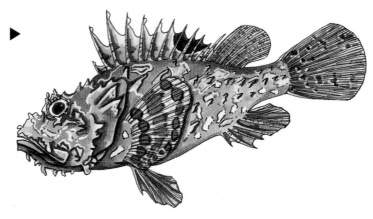

FAM. TRIGLIDAE

Grey gurnard
Eutrigla gurnardus

Fish with a body that is high in the front and tapering towards the tail. The head is long and concave with an almost straight and clearly oblique profile. The head is covered by strong bony plaques. The pectoral fins feature three lower rays that are free and very mobile. A long line of small spiny bony plaques runs along the flanks. Body colouration varies from olive grey to reddish brown on the back with a large number of whitish-yellow spots. The belly is whitish. This schooling species lives close to sandy and muddy sea-beds, at depths from 10 to 200 metres. In summer, this fish migrates inshore. It feeds on smaller fish, shrimp and crab. It can grow to a length of 45 cm.

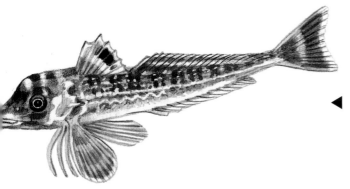

Tub gurnard
Trigla lucerna

A body that is high towards the front and slightly tapered towards the rear. The head, protected by bony lobes, presents a straight snout with a barely noticeable median incisure. The pectoral fins are very wide. Body colouration is generally brilliant and varies from red to reddish brown to yellowish with dark patches on the back. The sides are lighter, while the belly is whitish. This species lives close to sandy, muddy or detrital sea-beds, at depths from 5 –10 up to 300 metres. It is however also found in mid-water and has been seen jumping above the surface. It feeds mostly on lesser fish and can attain a length of 75 cm.

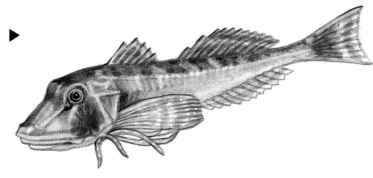

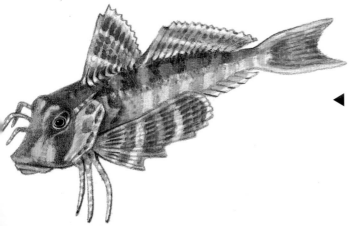

Red gurnard
Aspitrigla cuculus

Strong-bodied fish with a huge head covered by bony lobes. The snout has a concave frontal profile and bears 3-4 small spines on each side. The flanks are smooth. The pectoral fins are wide and their three lower rays are free. Body colouration is dark red on the back and silvery pink on the belly. This species lives close to sandy or detrital sea-beds as well as bottoms featuring sand and rocks, at depths varying between 20 and 250 metres. It feeds mostly on shrimp, crab and other benthic invertebrates as well as lesser fish. It can attain a length of 40 cm.

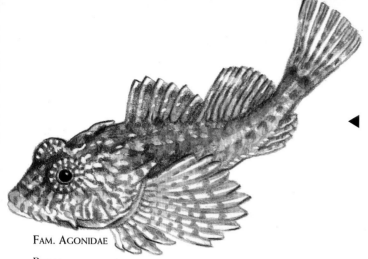

FAM. AGONIDAE

Pogge
Agonus cataphractus

Fish with a body featuring a tough armour of bony lobes. The large, triangular head is provided with a large number of short chin barbels. The two dorsal fins are closely placed. The pectoral fins are wide. Body colouration is brown with a few dark saddle-shaped patches on the back. The belly is yellowish white. This bottom dwelling species can be found at depths varying from a few metres to 200 metres, close to sandy and muddy sea-beds where it likes to lurk. It feeds on small crustaceans but is not averse to other invertebrates such as ophiurods, worms and molluscs. It can grow up to 20 cm in length.

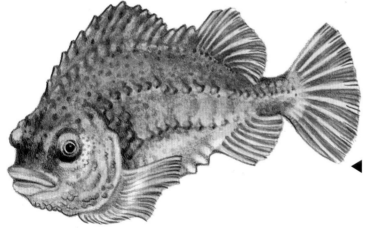

Sea snail
Liparis liparis

Small fish with slim and tapering body, reminiscent of tadpoles. It has a wide, rounded head. The dorsal and anal fins are long and linked to the tail fin. The pelvic fins are linked together and form a small round suction organ. The skin is soft and flaccid. Body colouration varies from yellowish to reddish brown, depending on the habitat of the fish. It lives in areas rich in seaweed or on sandy and muddy sea-beds, at depths varying between 5 and 150 m. It feeds on prawns, polychaetes and small fish. It can grow to a length of 18 cm.

FAM. COTTIDAE

Sea scorpion
Taurulus bubalis

A rather small but strong-bodied fish. The head is large with body crests and houses tough spines along the edges of the preoperculum. The skin is smooth and devoid of scales. This fish has two dorsal fins. The pelvic fins feature three rays. Body colouration varies depending on habitat, but most sea scorpions are greenish brown on the back and yellowish on the belly. This species lives close to rocky bottoms rich in algae, at depths between the surface and 30 metres. It feeds on small fish and crustaceans. Females can reach lengths of 18 cm.

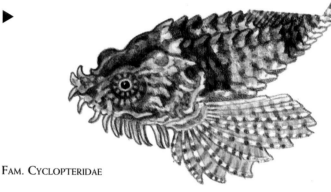

FAM. CYCLOPTERIDAE

Lumpsucker
Cyclopterus lumpus

A fish with a massive rounded body, covered by small dispersed bony knobs and four rows of larger bony knobs. The pelvic fins are close together and form a suction cup that the lumpsucker uses to anchor itself to the substrate. Body colouration is bluish grey, but in the spawning season, males take on an orange or reddish hue. This benthic species favours rocky sea-beds, at depths ranging from just a few metres to over 200 metres. It feeds on crustaceans, worms and lesser fish. It can attain a length of 60 cm. The eggs of this fish are marketed as a caviar substitute.

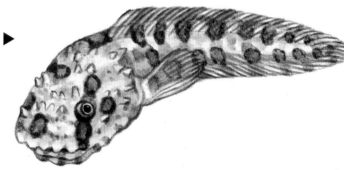

FAM. SERRANIDAE

Perch
Serranus cabrilla

Fish with a fairly elongated body that ends in a pointed snout. The front part of the dorsal fin features spine-like rays. The tail fin is concave. Body colouration is reddish brown, with a series of dark vertical bands intersected by yellow lines, even found on the head. It lives near various types of sea-bed (rocky, covered with seaweed, sandy) at depths varying from just a few metres to over 400 metres. It feeds on worms, crustaceans molluscs and lesser fish. This species is synchronically hermaphrodite, that is to say, it produces spermatozoa and eggs at the same time. It can reach a length of up to 30 cm.

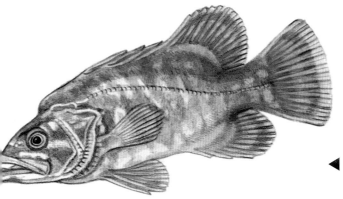

Wreckfish
Polyprion americanus

Heavy set fish with a pointed snout. The lower jaw protrudes markedly. The tail fin is rounded in juveniles and straight in adults. The pelvic fins are particularly developed and the first spine-like ray is very rough. Body colouration is purplish brown in juveniles and brownish in adults. Juveniles tend to swim in schools in mid-water while adults are solitary and favour a benthic habitat, especially close to wrecks at depths of about 30 to 40 metres. This species feeds on lesser fish and cuttlefish. Wreckfish can attain a length of up to 2 metres.

FAM. PERCICHTHYDAE

Bass
Dicentrachus labrax

Fish with a tapering profile and an almost straight back, featuring two clearly distinguishable dorsal fins. The upper jaw tends to project slightly over the lower jaw. The operculum features two spines. The tail fin is noticeably concave. Body colouration is generally silvery, with a greenish grey back and a black spot on the operculum. This fish tends to be bottom dwelling and favours sandy or detrital sea-beds, interspersed by rocks. It is frequently found in lagoons and estuaries. It feeds mainly on lesser fish. It can attain a length of 1 metre.

FAM. CARANGIDAE

Horse mackerel
Trachurus trachurus

Fish with a tapering, hydro-dynamic body that ends in very fine tail stump. The snout is pointed, with a prominent jaw and large eyes. The lateral line is very evident because it features scutes provided with carenae and a spine. Body colouration is iridescent green on the back and silvery on the belly. There is a black spot on the operculum. This schooling species is found in pelagic waters. The juveniles, especially, can be found inshore, generally associated with large jellyfish. It feeds on lesser fish and crustaceans. It can reach a length of 50 cm.

Amberjack
Seriola dumerili

Fish with a hydro-dynamic body, fine tail stump and sickle-shaped tail fin. The ogival head is rounded. Body colouring is blue–grey on the back while the flanks and belly feature yellow hues. A longitudinal yellow bank runs along the flanks while the eyes are separated by a dark stripe that extends up to the nape of the neck. This schooling species tends to come inshore in late spring and summer, favouring promontories and islands. It feeds on fish, crustaceans and cuttlefish. It can attain a length of 2 metres.

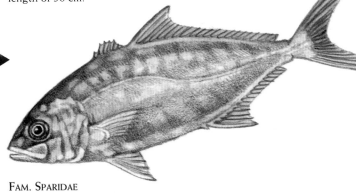

FAM. SPARIDAE

Pandora
Pagellus erythrinus

Fish with a fairly tapering body, small head and pointed snout. The mouth is large and features well-developed front teeth. The pectoral fins are pointed. The tail fin is sharply cut and forked. Body colouring is red orange on the back and flanks, gradually becoming lighter towards the belly that features silvery hues. This bottom dwelling species favours rock, sandy or detrital sea-beds, at depths varying between 20 and 100 m. It feeds on fish, small crustaceans and benthic molluscs. It can reach a length of 50 cm.

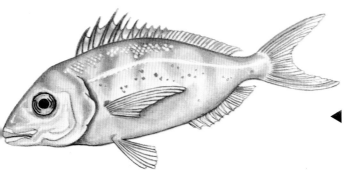

Gilthead
Sparus aurata

Fish with a massive, oval body that ends in a convex-shaped head. The upper jaw protrudes slight beyond the lower jaw. This species has rather large, canine and molar teeth. The pectoral fins are long and pointed. The tail fin is wide and clear-cut. Body colouration is greyish on the back and more silvery on the flanks. A black and golden coloured bank runs between the eyes. This bottom dwelling fish favours sandy or mixed sea-beds, at depths from just a few metres to over 30 metres. It feeds on molluscs and crustaceans. It grinds the shells of its prey with its strong teeth. It can grow up to 70 cm in length.

FAM. SCIAENIDAE

Argyrosomus regius

Fish with an elongated body covered with large scales. The head is relatively small and the edges of the preoperculum are indented. The tail fin has a straight edge. Body colouration is silvery brown on the back and lighter on the flanks that feature golden hues. The inside of the mouth is golden yellow. It lives close to sandy sea-beds and also ventures into fresh water. It feeds on small benthic fish such as sardines and mullet. It can reach a length of 2 m.

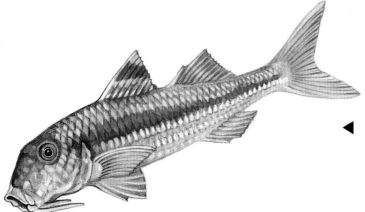

Black sea bream
Spondyliosoma cantharus

Deep oval body with a small head and smallish mouth, featuring well-developed fore teeth. Juveniles have a pointed snout, that is blunted in adults. The dorsal fin can be folded into an opening on the back. Body colouring is brown–grey on the back and lighter on the sides that bear about fifteen golden longitudinal lines. This species lives close to rocky sea-beds and wrecks, at depths varying from 8-10 metres to over 60 metres. The eggs are typically laid in holes in the sea-bed, dug by the male. It feeds on lesser fish and invertebrates. It can reach a length of up to 50 cm.

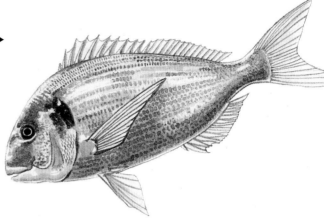

Pagellus acarne

Fish with an oval, elongated body and fairly convex back. The snout is thickset and the mouth wide. The jaws are of equal size, featuring small front teeth. Body colouring is pinkish on the back and slivery on the flanks and belly. The fins are reddish and the inside of the mouth is golden coloured or orange. There is a black spot at the base of the pectoral fins. This bottom dwelling fish is found close to sandy or muddy sea-beds at depths varying between 10 to about 100 metres. It feeds on crustaceans and other invertebrates. It can reach a length of 35 cm.

FAM. MULLIDAE

Red mullet
Mullus surmuletus

Fish with a deep front body, tapering rear body and almost straight belly. The head has a marked oblique profile. The protrusible mouth is located low on the head. The chin bear the two barbels typical of mullets. The tail fin is forked. Body colouring is reddish brown on the back, while the lighter flanks feature a red longitudinal band and yellow lines. The first dorsal fin has two dark transversal bands. This fish lives in small shoals close to rocky sea-beds, at depths from just a few metres to over 100 metres. It feeds on small benthic invertebrates. It can attain a length of 40 cm.

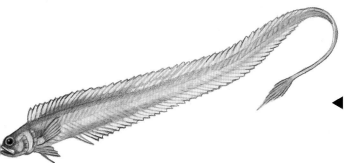

Cepola rubescens

This band-shaped fish has a compressed body that ends in a thin, pointed tail. The snout is short with large eyes and an oblique mouth with curved teeth. The dorsal fin starts at the gills and extends up to the tail fin. Body colouring is red, with a darker colour on the back. The dorsal and anal fins are yellow while the tail fin is red. It lives at depths varying between 15 and 100 m. close to muddy and detrital sea-beds into which it digs vertical dens. It leaves its den to prey on small planctonic crustaceans. It can grow to a length of 70 cm.

FAM. LABRIDAE

Ballan wrasse
Labrus bergylta

Fish with a well-built, rather deep and elongated body. It has a long pointed snout that ends in a rather small mouth. The rear edges of the preoperculum is smooth. Body colouring is very variable: red, greenish, brown, marbled or uniform, sometimes dotted with whitish spots. It lives close to rocky sea-beds and bottoms overgrown with laminaria, from depths varying from the tidal band to over 50 metres. It feeds on molluscs and crustaceans. It can attain a length of 60 cm.

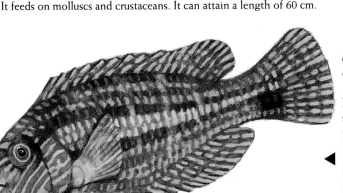

Luckoo wrassse
Labrus bimaculatus

Fish with a rather tapering body, elongated head and pointed snout. The mouth is wide. The rear edges of the preoperculum are smooth. Body colouration varies in function of sex: females and juvenile males are pinkish or reddish with 2-3 black spots at the base of the soft rays of the dorsal fin. Adult males have a greenish colouring on the front of the body, while the rear portion and belly are yellow and the head, brown. This species lives close to rocky sea-beds at depths varying between 10 m and over 150 m. It feeds on crustaceans, molluscs and worms. During the spawning season, males prepare a nest on the sea-bed. This fish can grow to a length of 35 cm.

Corkwing wrasse
Crenilabrus melops

Fish with a deep, oval body that ends in a short snout. The mouth is small with thin lips. The edge of the preoperculum is indented. The pelvic fins are long. Body colouring depends on sex: females are brown with dark spots and a greyish white belly. The irises of females are golden coloured or brown. Males are reddish brown with blue and green hues and stripes as well as red and orange spots. The irises of males are orange and green. This bottom dwelling species favours rocky sea-beds, rich in seaweed, at depths from varying from mid-tide to 30 metres. It can attain a length of 25 cm.

Goldsinny
Ctenolabrus rupestris

Fish with a rather slender body and pointed head featuring a small mouth with canine front teeth. The preoperculum is finely indented along its rear edge. Body colouration is variable: brown, orange or green, with dark bands along the flanks, a typical black spot on the upper part of the tail stump and another at the beginning of the dorsal fin. It feeds on crustaceans, snails, limmets and other small invertebrates. It can attain a length of up to 18 cm.

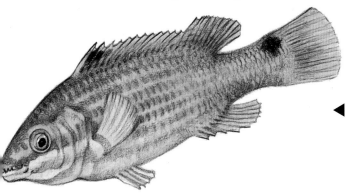

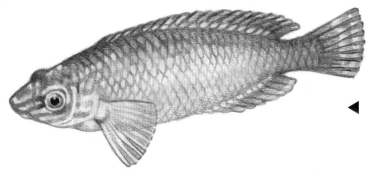

FAM. TRACHINIDAE

Greater weever
Trachinus draco

Elongated, compressed body with rather straight dorsal and ventral profiles. The snout is short and the mouth large, oblique and protrusible. The eyes are positioned towards the top of the head. The dorsal fin features tough dark spines that are attached to venom glands and therefore dangerous to the touch. The tail fin is slightly concave. Body colouration is greenish brown on the back, while the flanks are yellow white with bluish and yellowish spots and oblique lines. This fish has benthic habits and tends to lie buried in sandy sea-beds, with only the top of its head and spines of the dorsal fin above the sand. It feeds on smaller fish and crustaceans. It can grow to a length of up to 40 cm.

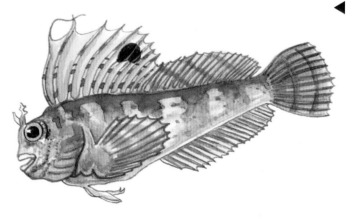

Tompot blenny
Parablennius gattorugine

Fish with an elongated body with a compressed rear portion. The snout is short and rounded. There is a pair of tentacles over the eyes. The mouth is large. The dorsal fin extends over most of the back. Body colouring is reddish grey with vertical dark bands that extend from the sides even up to the fins. It lives on rocky sea-beds rich in algae, from depths varying between 1-2 m and over 12 m. It feeds mainly on crustaceans. It can reach a length of 30 cm.

Rock cook
Centrolabrus exoletus

Moderately deep-bodied fish with an oval head. The mouth is small but features thick lips and small teeth arranged in a single row. The preoperculum is indented. Body colouration is greenish brown or reddish on the back, lighter on the flanks and yellowish on the belly. Males have blue spots on the fins and on the sides of the head. This bottom dwelling fish lives close to rocky sea-beds rich in algae, at depths varying from a just a few metres to 25 metres. It feeds on crustaceans, snails, limmets and other small invertebrates. This wrasse also behaves as a cleaner fish. It can reach a length of 15 cm.

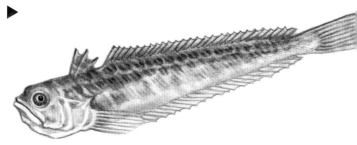

FAM. BLENNIDAE

Butterfly blenny
Blennius ocellaris

Fish with a deep, laterally compressed body. The snout is short, with an almost vertical profile. There are well-developed tentacles above the large eyes. This fish is unmistakeably identifiable by its large dorsal fin that has very long fore rays and a large eye-shaped black spot. Body colouration is yellowish or reddish white with brown vertical bands and dark longitudinal lines running along the lower part of the flanks. It lives close to detrital sea-beds at depths varying between 10 m and over 100 m. It feeds on crustaceans, polychaetes and fish. It can attain a length of 20 cm.

Shanny
Lipophrys pholis

Well-built body with a slightly convex back and almost straight belly. The head is rounded and totally devoid of tentacles. The mouth is rather large. The long dorsal fin features a slight depression separating the part made up of spiny rays from the rest, made up of soft rays. Body colouring varies from greenish brown to yellowish brown with a dark spot on the dorsal fin. This bottom dwelling fish favours rocky as well as sandy sea-beds, always rich in seaweed, at depths up to 30 metres below the surface. It feeds on small crustaceans including acorn barnacles. It can grow to 16 cm in length.

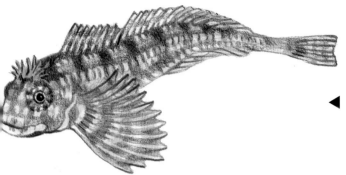

FAM. ANARHICHIDAE

Atlantic wolffish
Anarhicas lupus

Fish with a very well-built body that tapers markedly towards the tail. The head is high with a rounded snout and a wide mouth bearing large curved teeth, positioned on the front part of the jaw. There is a single dorsal fin that covers a large part of the back. There are no pelvic fins. Body colouring is brownish with dark mottling on the back and sides. This species lives close to rocky sea-beds interspersed with mud, at depths between 30 and 300 metres. It feeds on crab, molluscs and sea urchins. It can attain a length of 1.2 m.

FAM. AMMODYTIDAE

Lesser sandeel
Ammodytes tobianus

Fish with an elongated, tapering body featuring a sharp snout. It has a prominent lower jaw and protrusible mouth. The dorsal fin is very long, while the tail fin is small and forked. Body colouration is greenish yellow on the back, yellow on the flanks and silvery on the belly. This benthic schooling species lives close to sandy sea-beds, from the low tide level to depths of about 30 metres. It generally buries itself in the sand. It feeds on small invertebrates. It can attain a length of 20 cm.

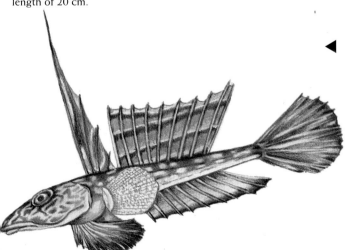

Montagu's blenny
Coryphoblennius galerita

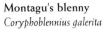

Well-developed body that tapers slightly towards the tail. The snout is straight and oblique. A typical crest of lappets runs between the eyes and along the middle of the head. Body colouring is olive brown with dark vertical bands. The lappet crest is orange in males. It lives close to rocky sea-beds, especially in intertidal waters. It can reach a length of 8 cm.

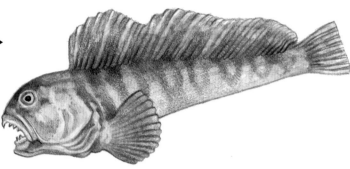

FAM. PHOLIDAE

Butterfish
Pholis gunnellus

Compressed, elongated body with a small head and rounded snout. The mouth features fleshy lips. The first dorsal fin runs up to the mid-point of the tail fin. The pelvic fins are reduced to just a few rays. Body colouring is greenish–brown, with vertical bands on the flanks. This species is distinguished by a row of ocellated dark coloured eye spots with white edges, located underneath the dorsal fin.
This species can be found from intertidal waters up to depths of 100 metres, close to rocky sea-beds. It feeds on polychaetes, small crustaceans and molluscs. It can attain a length of 25 cm.

FAM. CALLIONYMIDAE

Common dragonet
Callionymus lyra

Fish with flattened, elongated body. The head is large and the snout long. The lower jaw is slightly shorter than the upper jaw. The preoperculum features four spines: three point upwards while the most developed spine points forwards. In males, the first dorsal fin is higher than in females, with a very developed first ray. Colouration is brownish with side mottling that is darker in females. Males have light blue spots and stripes. This species lives close to sandy and muddy bottoms, at depths varying between 20 and over 100 m. It feeds on polychaetes, crustaceans and molluscs. While males can attain a length of 30 cm, females generally do not exceed 20 cm.

Black goby
Gobius niger

Fish with a well-built, stocky body, large, wide head, puffed lips and short snout. The eyes project from top part of the head. The tail fin is rounded. The first dorsal fin has elongated rays, especially in adult males. Colouration is grey brown with yellow hues and dark blotches and spots, even on the fins. It feeds on small crustaceans, polychaetes, mollsucs and fish. It can attain a length of 17 cm.

Rock goby
Gobius paganellus

Fish with a moderately strong body, that is deep in the front. The tail stump is large, and the tail fin rounded. The pectoral fins have a well distinguished fringe of free upper rays. Colouration is brown with dark blotches on the back and fins. Adult males have purplish hues and an orange band on the first dorsal fin. Found mainly near rocky bottoms rich in seaweed, below the low water mark up to depths of 15 m., this fish is not uncommon intertidally. It feeds on small crustaceans and fish. It can grow to a length of 12 cm.

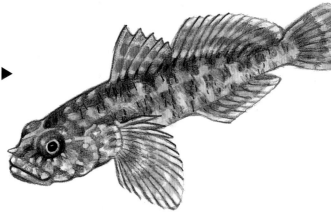

Giant goby
Gobius cobitis

Fish with a stocky body and deep tail stump. The head is large and prominent on the sides. The lips are well developed. The eyes project from the back. The upper rays of the dorsal fin are free. The pelvic fins are linked by an undulated membrane that forms two lobes. Colouration is olive brown with brown blotches. Odd-numbered fins have light borders. This species is most commonly found intertidally, close to rocky and detrital bottoms. It feeds on algae and crustaceans. It is the largest species of the goby family and can attain a length of 27 cm.

Leopard-spotted goby
Thorogobius ephippiatus

Fish with a relatively tapering body that ends in a deep and long tail stump. The head is compressed. The eyes project from the back. The tail fin is truncated, with rounded edges. Body colouration is whitish with orange or reddish shots. The first dorsal fin features a black spot at the base, while the pectoral fins have two orange blotches. This species lives at depths between 5 and 40 m, near steep rocky bottoms where it hides in fissures and holes. It feeds mainly on crustaceans and polychaetes. It can attain a length of 13 cm.

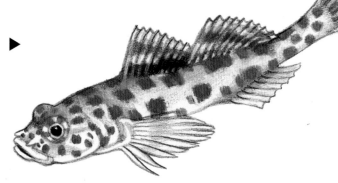

Mackerel
Scomber scombrus

Fish with a tapering, hydro-dynamic body, pointed snout and thin tail. Both the upper and lower edges feature finlets that support a well-defined fin. The eyes are characterised by large fatty eyelids. Body colouration is metallic iridescent blue–green on the back with sinuous lateral lines on the upper part of the silvery white flanks. This schooling pelagic species tends to come inshore during the summer months. It feeds on pelagic crustaceans and small schooling fish such as herring, sardines and sandeels. It can attain a length of 66 cm.

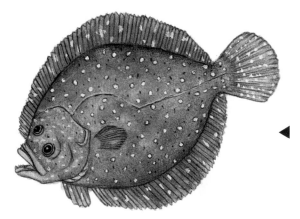

FAM. PLEURONECTIDAE

Dab
Limanda limanda

Fish with a very compressed, oval body and small mouth. The eyes are on the right side. The lateral line is markedly curved above the pectoral fin. The body is rough, covered by finely indented scales. The camouflage colouring of this fish is basically greyish or yellowish–brown with typical orange coloured mottling. Bottom-dwelling, it is found at depths varying from just a few metres to 150 metres. It feeds on crustaceans, small fish, molluscs and echinodermatous species (starfish). It can attain a length of 42 cm.

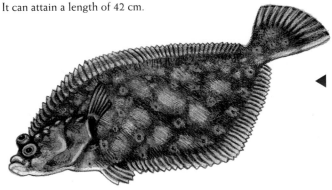

FAM. SOLEIDAE

Sole
Solea vulgaris

Fish with a flat, oval body and eyes on the right side. The head has a rounded profile. The mouth is small and curved. The dorsal and anal fins are linked by a membrane to the tail. Body colouring is more or less light brown with irregular blotches. The pectoral fin has a dark spot on the upper half It lives close to sandy and muddy bottoms at depths from 10 to 150 metres. It feeds mainly on crustaceans, polychaetes and molluscs but it can also catch small fish. It can attain a length of 60 cm.

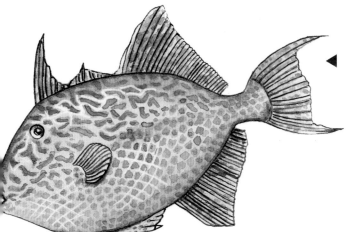

FAM. SCOPHTHALMIDAE

Turbot
Scophthalmus maximus

Fish with a compressed, disc-shaped body and eyes on the left side, position almost one above the other. The first rays of the dorsal fin are branched and free. The body is interspersed with large bony knobs. The colouration is very camouflaged, but is basically brown with light and dark blotches. Bottom-dwelling, it prefers detrital and sandy sea-beds, at depths ranging between 5 and 70 metres. It feeds on small fish such as sandeels, small codfish, goby, herring and sprat. It can attain a length of 1 metre.

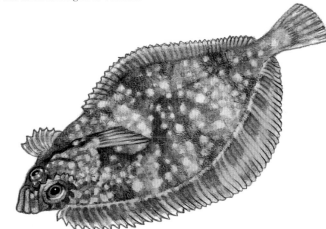

Plaice
Pleuronectes platessa

Fish with a compressed, oval body and small eyes on the right side. The lateral line is slightly curved above the pectoral fin. The body is smooth, although there is a series of body knobs running from lateral line to the eyes. It lives close to sandy and detrital or shingle covered bottoms, at depths varying from just a few metres to 200 m. It feeds on crustaceans and polychaetes. It can attain a length of 90 cm.

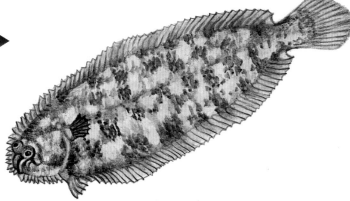

FAM. BALISTIDAE

Trigger fish
Balistes carolinensis

Fish with a deep, compressed and subquadrangular body covered with thick, rough scales. It has a conic snout and a mouth with tough conic teeth. The first dorsal fin features spiny rays of different lengths. The tail fin is crescent-shaped in adults, with very long upper and lower rays. Body colouring is greyish with greenish or blue hues and undulated lines on the fins. This bottom dwelling species lives close to rocky sea-beds at depths ranging from 5-7 metres to over 100 metres, coming inshore in the summer. It feeds on crustaceans and molluscs. It can attain a length of 40 cm.

Cover
A diver swims near a colony of yellow alcyonaria at Le Taureau in Brittany.
Photograph by Yves Gladu

Back cover – top
Spiny star fish are typical of the sea bed at Douarnenez Bay in Brittany.
Photograph by Yves Gladu

Back cover – centre
The wreck of the Brummer.
Drawing by Mariano Valsesia/White Star archive

Back cover – bottom
A juvenile saithe looks for shelter among stinging tentacles.
Photograph by Lawson Wood

168 Like the squid, the cuttlefish (Seppia officinalis) is one of the oldest classes of animal in the world. It lives in nearly all the seas around the world.

PHOTOGRAPHIC CREDITS